Amirtharaj Christy Williams is a wildlife biologist who started his academic career working for a Ph.D. on elephants in the Rajaji-Corbett landscape in Uttarakhand. Since then he has been working for over two decades to save Asian elephants across several range countries from India in the west to Malaysian Borneo in the east. His work has ranged from raising money to put boots on the ground to protect elephants to lobbying political leadership for policy changes that are elephant friendly. He is currently based in Saudi Arabia's NEOM region where he is involved in setting up a 2 million ha protected area. He has been a passionate advocate for wildlife conservation in general and is also an award-winning photographer. He is married to a wildlife biologist and they have two sons.

TIPU
Sultan of the Siwaliks

Amirtharaj Christy Williams

Speaking Tiger
YOUNG ADULT

SPEAKING TIGER BOOKS LLP
125A, Ground Floor, Shahpur Jat,
Near Asiad Village, New Delhi 110 049

First published in paperback in Speaking Tiger YA
by Speaking Tiger Books in 2021

ISBN: 978-93-5447-114-8

eISBN: 978-93-5447-122-3

10 9 8 7 6 5 4 3 2 1

Typeset in Alegreyat by Jojy Philip
Printed at Sanat Printers, Kundli

Contents

Foreword

Elephants in Africa have long had their chroniclers, scientists and conservationists almost as charismatic as the species themselves—Ian Douglas Hamilton, Cynthia Moss, Joyce Poole, among others. Books and films based on long years of research humanised the African elephant, revealing their sentience, society, and intelligence; garnering support for the beleaguered giant.

Meanwhile, our Asian elephant, no less remarkable an animal lives—and dies—in the shadows.

India is home to 50 per cent of wild Asian elephants. Here, the elephant is in the everyday—a creature of myth, religion, folklore. Worshipped as Ganesha, evoked in our prayers. Yet, in the real world, most of what we hear and see is of elephants on 'rampage', caught in horrific conflict situations: elephants on the run, chased, hounded by agitated crowds; elephants destroying crops, killing people, and in turn, being beaten, bludgeoned, poisoned, or electrocuted to death.

The Asian elephants are in distress, slipping away, endangered, edging toward extinction... unheard, unsung.

The narratives of this bitter battle have mostly been one-sided. As author and wildlife biologist Christy Williams writes in this book, 'Despite my deep feelings of empathy for the humans impacted (by conflict), I know that it is the elephants who are losing the battle everywhere. Across Asia, their home, the forests, are rapidly being cleared for human use, forcing them into closer contact and confrontation with humans. No one meets with elephants to get stakeholder opinion on what it's like to lose their homes.'

Christy did. For five years, he lived among the elephants in Rajaji National Park, on the bank of the Ganga in the north Indian state of Uttarakhand. Eight elephants were fitted with radio collars—the largest ever study of its time in Asia—giving unique insights into their ecology and behaviour; and a window into the hidden life of elephants. Elephants don't talk, at least not in the way humans do. They use a language of rumbles, trumpets, squeaks, grunts, gestures—a sway of the trunk, a swish of the tail, a flap of the ears, rubbing of heads—it all has meaning, but only if we are attuned to it, if we open our minds and hearts.

Christy listened and believed. And he became their voice, interpreting for an unknowing public their stories of kinship and love; grief and joy. It is a story told from the elephants' perspective, with passion and underpinned with robust science.

The author followed and observed the pachyderms; his pioneering research established how elephants, especially with calves, are negatively affected by human disturbance, contesting the deeply entrenched position that elephants and people can co-exist peacefully in a perfectly balanced eco-system. The study in Rajaji went on for twenty-five years, while the author also followed the elephants across their range—in Myanmar, Nepal, Bhutan, Indonesia, Malaysian Borneo and Laos.

Christy is a keen student, and over the years he absorbs what it is to be an elephant. He learns how they communicate, warn each other of danger, send calls for help or to find other members of the group, and even to spread the good word, for example, where salt, a much-desired delicacy—can be had! He records their strong familial bonds, writing movingly about how they sacrifice their life for their children.

It's a fallacy to consign elephants into a 'single grey lump'. Each is an individual, with distinct personalities, idiosyncrasies and quirks. Like the irrepressible but gentlemanly Tipu, the protagonist of this book who couldn't resist sugarcane, but never harmed a soul in his daily—sorry—nightly crop raids. There are others readers will become acquainted with: the bold and wilful Diana, the gentle and wise matriarch Mallika.

Knowing elephants with an intimacy such as Christy's is a unique privilege, and in this book told with deep empathy and sharp humour, he lets us into the enigmatic world of the *Elephas maximus*.

As someone who works for a kinder, safe world for elephants, I can vouch that the elephants could not have asked for a stronger advocate, a more eloquent spokesperson than Christy. In writing this book, he honours the elephants, while making us reflect on our indifference, if not abuse, towards an animal akin to us. The reader will not be unaffected. For me, personally, the reading of *Tipu, the Sultan of the Siwaliks* is not an end, but marks the beginning of a deeper kinship with elephants. I hope it similarly leaves the reader with a conviction that like *Homo sapiens*, all animals, including elephants, deserve a life, and death, of dignity.

Prerna Singh Bindra

CHAPTER 1

How It Happened

I can close my eyes and recall the place, date and time when I received the email that set in motion the thoughts that ended in me writing this book. It was the sixth of April 2017 and I was in a double-decker tourist bus in Thailand. Along with nearly thirty of WWF Myanmar staff, we were driving to Bangkok airport to catch our flight back to Yangon, Myanmar. We had just spent three days in the Kui Buri and Kaeng Krachan National Parks and had seen elephants, gibbons, gaur, langurs and a myriad other wildlife and, for some of my colleagues, it had been their first ever encounter with real forests and wildlife. Everyone was happy and karaoke was in full swing over the public address system of the bus. It was a perfect setting and there was little indication of the dark clouds hanging over the future of elephants in Myanmar.

I pulled out my phone to check if we had network connection and it showed a strong 3G network signal. After nearly two days of not having been connected to the internet, it was time to check emails. I waited for the emails to download and was quickly overwhelmed by over 150 emails that had come in while I was off the net. As I scanned the subject lines of the emails, deciding whether to open and read, something caught my eye. It was an email from my colleague Aung Myo Chit, the head of the Myanmar office of The Smithsonian Conservation Biology Institute (SCBI). The subject was 'Delta Poaching'.

I clicked on it and it read, 'These pictures are from the delta and I am sending more in the next email'. Attached to the email were horrifying photos of dead elephants. Their skins had been completely removed and all you could see was dead and decaying pink flesh. I have seen many horrors during my twenty years of working on elephant research and conservation but this was on a totally different scale. I felt as if someone had punched me in my gut. I wanted to click the email shut, but I wasn't able to avert my eyes from the photos either. There were no words to express the alarm and dismay I felt right then. I passed the photos on to some of my WWF colleagues and replied to Aung saying, 'My god...this is really getting out of hand in Myanmar. Aung I am in office on Monday/Tuesday, please let us try and meet up.' To which I still remember Aung's immediate reply, 'Yes, we can proudly inform international wildlife conservation communities that "all the elephant will soon return to their creator"' and the attached photos including that of a young elephant lying dead and completely skinned.

The rest of the trip and flight home was a blur as I was experiencing something I had never felt before. The weekend that followed felt as if it wouldn't end, and living by myself in Yangon, I had no one to talk to. I felt helpless for the first time in my life. Anger was followed by a murderous rage towards poachers and people who supported illegal trade. Till that point in time, I had seen a few photos of dead elephants with skins neatly removed and I had thought these were rare, one-off cases rather than the main reason for elephant deaths. The photos of nearly ten dead elephants, all found in a short radius, possibly members of the same family brought home the reality that elephants could disappear in a blink if we didn't do something radically different.

At that point I realized that Asian elephants were slipping away without much of the civilized world being aware of how endangered they were.

The more visible plight of African elephants was simply overwhelming any attempt to highlight the predicament of Asian elephants. The threats African elephants faced was an easier story to tell as many of them live in open grassland savannah habitats and millions of tourists visit every year to see them in famous national parks mainly in southern and eastern Africa. There were a lot of disturbing photos and videos of African elephants being butchered for their tusks, and several films have come out talking about the ivory trade and the slaughter of elephants in Africa. Charismatic individuals (both researchers and wildlife wardens) have written intimate stories about their connections to the elephants they have studied or whose lives they defended in the face of poachers. In some cases, these real-life stories have made into the living rooms of people far away in the form of television documentaries thus building a big constituency of concerned people who were forced to act either through their chequebooks or through other means including lobbying their politicians to take action to stop the slaughter. Several billionaires and western governments have invested millions of dollars trying to save the African elephants.

In contrast, except in a few sites in south Asia, Asian elephants are hard to see as they live in forests and are quite shy. So, barring the few places where Asian elephants can be observed peacefully in their natural habitat, much of their recent photos have been of them involved in conflict situations being chased by humans or run over by speeding trains. The situation was also complicated by the fact that maybe about thirty per cent of Asian elephants left are in captivity.

So when a tourist comes to Asia, it is highly likely they will see a captive elephant sometime during their trip. This makes it appear that elephants are everywhere and there is no danger of them disappearing from the earth. There are parks in Southeast Asia where there are more captive elephants than wild ones, a fact hard to believe. Added to this mix was the lack of books or documentaries of charismatic individuals telling the story of Asian elephants as individuals.

Very few researchers have had the opportunity to study Asian elephants intimately and follow them over multiple years. I was lucky to get this rare chance because in 1994 my supervisor at the Wildlife Institute of India at Dehradun, A.J.T. Johnsingh (AJT), wanted scientific information to back up his life's mission of restoring Rajaji National Park to its pristine state.

Rajaji National Park had been overrun with humans when I first went there to study elephants. The Park had been fragmented into two pieces by a road, a rail track and an ammunition dump. AJT was the only scientist who had consistently argued for the need to remove humans to create a disturbance free zone for the elephants and tigers and to restore the corridor so that they could move easily across the Ganges. This was his life's mission. My contribution towards that goal was going to be finding out what influences how an elephant decides to move, feed and survive by collaring eight individual elephants, the largest radio-collaring effort in Asia at that time.

At the same time, some powerful voices were arguing that humans and elephants have lived in a perfectly balanced ecosystem in Rajaji and that we scientists, with ideas derived from Western education, were trying to disturb this. They also claimed there was no evidence to show that humans were negatively affecting the elephants in the Park. As a scientist it was my job to collect data and see which of these two competing hypotheses were true.

It was a challenging but enjoyable assignment. In the end it was clear from the data that disturbance has a major influence on movement and habitat use for elephants. Female elephants with calves did not tolerate disturbance at all and they responded to it by moving into areas with fewer cattle, but also less food. Thus, resettling Gujjar communities outside the Park area had to be given priority. More areas in the Park had to be freed up of human disturbance if we wanted elephants to survive in the long term. Gradually, it was gratifying to see more scientific evidence coming in to back up AJT's arguments. Finally he found an ally in A.S. Negi, who became the head of the Uttarakhand Forest Department a few years after I left to take a job with WWF in Nepal. The process of freeing up Rajaji from human disturbance and to strengthen the connectivity across the Ganga river started in earnest.

Seventeen years later, the heart-rending photos of dead and skinned elephants arrived in my inbox. I felt guilty that apart from publishing scientific papers I had not made any effort to tell the larger world about the elephants of Rajaji and what they taught me. I had been given a very rare opportunity and a first-hand glimpse into their daily lives for five years and I had failed to honour my debt to them by not writing about their wonderful behavioural qualities.

I had been working on Asian elephants for nearly twenty-five years and everything I had achieved had begun because of those elephants in Rajaji who I got to know intimately and who allowed me to observe and learn about them first hand and not from some book. I felt that, apart from my day-to-day work in conservation, it was my duty to tell the stories about these wonderful social animals whose family bonding could put us to shame. So I searched for and found my old my notebooks and dusted them and sat down to write this book. I hope that you will feel a spirit of kinship with all elephants, Asian and African, after you read the story of my life with the elephants in Rajaji National Park.

CHAPTER 2

Moving North

I woke up shivering and rummaged for things to keep me warm. Finding nothing appropriate except for a bunch of shirts to wrap around my rapidly freezing feet and hands, I started cursing no one in particular for not informing me about winters in north India. It was December 1993. I hadn't even brought shoes and socks! Icy condensation dripped on me. If I didn't make it through the night, my body at least would be well preserved in the morning.

My journey started from warm and steamy Madras (now known as Chennai), where the temperature was always at a comfortable 35 degrees Celsius. It wasn't that I was not used to cold weather. I had grown up in the tea estates of the Blue Mountains of Western Ghats where temperatures plunge to two to three degrees in the winter. There, however, we had always been prepared with warm clothing and a nice wood fire or an electric heater.

On the train to Delhi, everything was dark and not a soul stirred. As if the cold was not bad enough, this was the first time I was travelling north of Bangalore into the Hindi-speaking heartland and I didn't know a word of Hindi.

I had seen an advertisement seeking Research Fellows at the Wildlife Institute of India (WII), Dehradun, a new and premier institute for wildlife research at that time. My friend Yoganand (Yogi) and I decided to apply and made arrangements to reach Dehradun in time for the entrance tests. Arrangements were duly made, tickets were booked and the day to leave for Delhi arrived.

Yogi, with whom I had been studying in Pondicherry for an MS degree in Ecology for the past two years, was a strong believer in not arriving for any kind of public transport unless it had already pulled out of the station. He even arrived late to catch the ship that was to take him to the Andaman Islands for his MS thesis work on birds, and only made it as the gangplank was being lifted. Another friend threw Yogi's suitcase onto the deck as he scrambled across the gangplank, suspended in mid-air.

With a friendship that entailed many such instances of being forced into last-minute sprints at various bus stands and train stations, I had come to realize that it was not good for my heart and had this time insisted on being the one to hold the tickets for the journey. In fact, I intended to have a ringside view, from inside the train, of him doing the mad dash.

True to form, as the train started pulling out of the station in Madras, there was no sign of Yogi. I was leaning out of the door, scanning the station platform with anxiety, when I saw him ambling like a bear at the far end of the platform. I yelled. It would be an understatement to say it was touch and go with him having made it into one of the rear compartments with only 20 feet of platform left for the train to clear. With his practised ease, he shuffled into sight with a grin and nary a sign of stress while I breathlessly collapsed into my seat.

So there we were travelling together, not knowing what the future held for us. As luck would have it, a female friend, on whom Yogi had a secret crush, was in the seat opposite us. His heart was broken when we found out that she was travelling with her boyfriend.

That first night of the journey, the cold already seeping into my bones, I looked down and across to the berth Yogi was sleeping in. As my eyes adjusted to the dim light thrown by the night lamp, I was surprised to find him sitting with a morose look on his face. On following his eyes, I peered under my berth and saw our common friend and her boyfriend snuggling together, for warmth, with a blanket wrapped around them.

My teeth started to chatter and my limbs were numb. The next morning, I was livid when I discovered that Yogi had an unused blanket tucked away in his suitcase. With fate having thrown a wet blanket on the matters of his heart, the actual cold didn't seem to have the slightest effect on him. Of course I had no such protection from the elements and had to endure the torturous journey till we reached Dehradun the next day.

We spent the rest of the week writing the entrance test and attending an interview while walking around spellbound by the gleaming new buildings of the Institute. In the glitzy computer room and library, there were rows of shiny computers. I had come from a lab where we had to work in shifts on a few battered computers, only recently upgraded from punch cards—the way to program code into computers in the early days before floppy diskettes and keyboards.

What really clinched my decision to join if offered a place, however, happened on the first freezing morning at the Institute when there was a knock on the door. It was Dinesh, the mess boy, standing there, greeting me with a cup of steaming hot tea. I decided that this was my absolute ideal of how wildlife research should be conducted. Later that morning I was offered one of the twenty fellowships. I joined immediately.

Before we came to Dehradun to join the Institute, both Yogi and I had been carrying out research work in the field. While Yogi had been away studying birds on islands, I was helping out with large mammal research in Mudumalai Wildlife Sanctuary in Tamil Nadu, focusing on how elephants and other larger mammals like deer and sloth bears helped in dispersing seeds of plants by eating their fruit. The work involved a lot of digging through animal dung and scat—something my mother always tried to hide from our relatives. She would quickly change the subject whenever someone asked me for more details about my research. Several of my cousins were just entering the lucrative field of technology and the last thing she wanted was her son describing how he rummaged through animal shit as a career path.

After completing six months of research on seed dispersal by large mammals, I continued working as a research assistant for Dr. Sukumar at the Indian Institute of Science, studying gaur, an attractive species of wild cattle. The year I had spent in Mudumalai, before this trip, had given me plenty of opportunities to observe wild elephants from a distance and I spent many hours watching them in fascination. I wanted to study elephants if I ever got a chance.

I then went to meet Dr. Johnsingh, known to all as AJT, India's first large mammal biologist. We discussed whether I should study the ecology of gorals, a mountain antelope, or elephants for my Ph.D. I suspect that at the time he wanted me to study gorals, but he suggested that I go and spend a couple of days exploring Rajaji National Park, an hour away from the Institute, before I returned to Bangalore to submit my resignation from the project I was working on. The next afternoon a vehicle was arranged and I was on my way to Dholkhand, the camp in Rajaji, where the Institute's field station for research was based.

My only experience of forests with wild elephants, at that time, was the Mudumalai–Bandipur complex in south India where I had been working. That landscape was filled with vast teak and bamboo forests, scrub jungles and semi-evergreen patches interspersed with swampy grasslands, quite unlike the forests in south India that conveyed a sense of permanence.

There were no eroding hills and changing river courses there.

As we drove through the forests to Dholkhand, I was able to see the forests I planned to work in over the next few years. Rajaji nestled in the Siwalik hills. A ridgeline ran like a spine along the middle of the long park dividing it into the northern part that connected to Doon valley, and the southern part where hills merged abruptly into the plains of Uttar Pradesh. The Ganges river separated the western part of the Park from the eastern part. A narrow corridor, now completely occupied by villages and an army cantonment, connected the two sides across the Ganges. The hillsides were clothed with grass and shrubs and a few scattered trees that had been completely stripped off their green twigs except for a few unreachable twigs on the top. The relatively flatter areas seemed to be dominated by tall sal trees, a valuable timber species.

Even more disconcerting were the dry riverbeds, called rau, filled with smooth white boulders. These dissected the park at regular intervals. One could see that erosion was a fact of life here, with steep hillsides, rising above these raus, constantly being reshaped every monsoon by the rushing floods. I felt a sense of great temporariness in this place where several forces of nature hadn't finished their task of shaping these hills. It appeared that the physical features of hills and the river courses were constantly changing.

Gujjars, a once nomadic group of pastoralists, added their presence to this rapidly evolving landscape nearly ninety years ago. They have now settled permanently with their milch buffaloes, adding their voices and buffalo bells to the chaotic cacophony of the area. They were everywhere, and their yelling and singing along with the sounds of the wooden bells around the buffalo necks were heard long before they were seen.

My head was whirling and I repeatedly asked myself whether this was what I really wanted to do. I had imagined carrying out elephant research in pristine wilderness with vast undisturbed forests. My reverie was broken with our arrival in Dholkhand which was less disturbed than the areas we had passed through.

Ramesh and Ram Sharan, two siblings who worked as field assistants for the Institute's projects met me there. The driver said goodbye and drove off. I picked up my bag and followed the brothers to their one-room lodging, plonked down on a charpoy and gratefully drank the very sweet hot tea they offered me. The Institute employed a bunch of field assistants and the seniormost among them, Yasin, came to give me a background about the Park. All research fellows were helped by the assistants to carry out research work. Some of them knew Rajaji like the back of their hands as they had been working in the Park for over a decade. Later that night, with only a small kerosene lamp for light, I ate a frugal but tasty dinner before falling asleep.

The next day, I was up and ready before sunrise and eager to get going. I wanted to walk around to get a feeling for the forests and the wildlife there. It was bitterly cold and a slight mist hovered over the forest. A second cup of tea later, it was decided that Yasin and I would trek up the goral ridge to, what else but, see gorals in the morning.

As the morning rays of the sun struggled through the foreboding grey sky, we started our trek into the hills. I could hear the calls of several birds, drowned out by the cackling call of the oriental pied hornbills and the *pheaou...pheaou* of the peafowl.

With the jacket I had purchased in Delhi zipped up tightly, Yasin and I climbed higher and higher in search of gorals, a mammal I had never seen. My recent readings had revealed that many people thought the goral had gone extinct locally until AJT started to climb these ridges and pointed them out to all and sundry. We must have been climbing for about thirty minutes when somewhere midway up the ridge we spotted a goral standing near the top, looking down into the sal forests below.

In the early morning light, the goral had not spotted us. While I was trying to look at it through Yasin's binoculars, I noticed a sudden movement on the face of the hill and saw two sambar deer foraging in the grass. I was happy to see two mammals within such a short space of time. But more importantly, the goral and sambar sighting allowed me to catch my breath after an exhausting climb.

Soon after, we reached a steep portion of the ridge where there was a foot-wide path that was disintegrating with every step. By then I was like the goral and sambar I had seen—down on four limbs to prevent myself from slipping and falling. Also, I was totally breathless.

Meanwhile, Yasin was skipping lightly ahead as if we were walking on a broad flat road. He pretended to be oblivious to the tall and undernourished researcher from south India who looked like he would not last the climb to the top.

Suddenly, Yasin stopped to point out a tree on a gentle slope on the far side of the ridge. I saw a troop of grey langurs sitting on it surrounded by ten to fifteen chital deer. I immediately put to shame all primate and deer researchers as I stood there, chest heaving with great breaths, pretending to observe the animals' every move intently. I continued this act for a very long time. I even pulled out my notebook and pretended to take notes. Since that day, I've been eternally thankful to langurs and chital for buying me the time, on a steep ridge, to get back my breath and bearings and not lose face.

It occurred to me, much later, that Yasin might have contrived this break to save himself the trouble of carrying me back down the slope. We stood rooted to the spot until I had sufficiently recovered, then finished our climb to the top and started descending on the other side. While climbing down, we startled a barking deer and a group of rhesus macaques. It had been an exciting day filled with wildlife.

I had already made up my mind, somewhere early on the way up that confounded ridge, that goral was not my cup of tea. Climbing ridges everyday did not fit into my idea of how wildlife research should be conducted. Little did I know that elephants in Rajaji were actually fat gorals in disguise. In subsequent years, I would spend many hours climbing these blasted ridges behind them.

After a simple meal of rotis and dal and a brief rest that afternoon, I set off with Ram Sharan in search of elephants. We set off on foot on a small path into a mixed sal forest with a shrub-filled understorey. The trees had all been fed on by elephants. Many branches were twisted, broken and hanging at odd angles. The trees and shrubs had the appearance of arrested growth, remaining at a certain height due to constant feeding by elephants.

We proceeded for about half an hour when we came to a *Mallotus philippensis* (Rohini) tree whose base was strewn with fresh leaves stripped neatly from the branches. I saw broken branches that were still wet, and the bark cleanly removed. Ram Sharan hurriedly whispered that the elephants must be nearby and that we should proceed with caution.

Usually, while tracking elephants in the forest, there is a period when your adrenaline starts pumping and you can feel the excitement flow through your veins. It triggers on encountering either fresh, steaming elephant dung, or wet twigs and leaves from a recent meal. It can happen upon hearing the crack of a twig, the flapping of great ears, a sigh between feeding pauses, or the sound of dust being blown out of a trunk.

You hold your breath and learn to walk softly, with extra attentive ears straining to catch any noise that would betray the presence of elephants. Then suddenly, your heart stops when you hear the loud crack of a tree in its final throes as it is pushed over by a bull somewhere really close. I came to love this feeling and have been hard pressed to find other activities where I feel this alive from breathless anticipation.

The signs were certainly there this afternoon. As we proceeded cautiously, I could feel every nerve in my body taut with tension. We stopped and listened for sounds, but could discern none that indicated elephants. I walked gingerly for fear of making any noise that would alert the elephants to our presence.

After about two hundred metres of this nerve-rackingly slow progress, we stopped at the sound of feeding. The visibility in the area was poor, dense with shrubs. The elephants were very close, but we couldn't see even a single bush move.

I could hear my heart pounding so loudly I was almost sure the elephants could hear it. We fell to our knees and gestured to each other to communicate, with Ram Sharan indicating that it would be best if we retreated from there because it was impossible to sight the elephants without disturbing them. All the while, I could hear the elephants clearly, including the flapping of their ears. It sounded like there was definitely more than one elephant, and felt it prudent to follow Ram Sharan's advice.

Just as we started to move away, the wind changed direction and, suddenly, all feeding sounds died away, followed by a deep throbbing call. Having worked with elephants in the Mudumalai forests in southern India, I immediately recognized that as the warning call to other elephants about the presence of danger.

That warning call quickened our steps. As we hurried from that place, we came to a big ficus tree. I indicated to Ram Sharan that we should climb it.

We must have been sitting on a branch about twelve feet above the ground when I heard the sound of feeding resume. We waited. Within minutes, a big female with a calf at heel, pushed through a *Mallotus* shrub on which she was feeding. She methodically removed the leaves on the small twigs before stuffing them into her mouth. The thicker branches she rotated in her mouth to loosen the outer bark and then delicately peeled the inner layer with the tip of her trunk before eating it.

All of a sudden, she stopped feeding and walked straight to our tree and stood underneath it. If I reached down I could have touched her back. I held my breath and could feel the hair on my arm stand on end from the excitement of being so close to such a large, wild animal. In a few moments, the mother and daughter moved away unhurriedly and resumed feeding. I did not know then that this would be the defining moment of my life. This was the day elephants happened to me.

I turned to Ram Sharan and saw that he had been holding his breath, too. Right there and then, over those adrenalin-induced abnormal heartbeats, Ram Sharan and I formed a bond that has now lasted over twenty years through hundreds of exciting encounters with elephants.

CHAPTER 3

Tipu, Sultan of the Siwaliks

After joining the Institute as a research fellow to study elephants, I was told that the government wanted more information about elephants in the Garo Hills in north-east India. AJT asked me to do this assignment as the information was needed urgently for formulating a conservation action plan. I agreed and spent a year studying elephants for the Government of India in the remote Garo Hills. This work led to some important conservation efforts including identifying important elephant ranges and critical corridors. I then came back to Rajaji and started my research on elephants. The plan was for me to collar eight elephants—four females and four solitary bulls and track them so we could answer important questions about their ecology. It took us almost a year to import the radio collars and get all the required permissions to capture and collar elephants. I was getting tired of all the waiting.

Then in December of 1995, the moment I had been waiting for finally arrived. AJT came one winter day to Rajaji with some forest officer trainees from the Institute. As they were leaving, he said, 'Christy, take a couple of field assistants and go to Motichur with the equipment.' Seeing the surprised look on my face, he continued, 'We now have the required permissions to collar four elephants. There is a bull near Raiwala town who has been raiding crops for the last two weeks and the Park Director of Rajaji wants us to collar him first.'

Raiwala was on the northern side of the Park, so I protested that it would be logistically impossible, let alone the fact that we did not have receivers or the money for petrol to track an elephant over that kind of distance. AJT cut me off before I could get very far with my complaints. 'We have to do this as a public relations exercise for the Forest Department.' So that was that. He was my boss, after all, and so I left for Motichur with Ram Sharan, another assistant named Meghraj, and a lot of apprehension.

An elephant collaring operation involved a lot of logistics. First the wild elephant had to be located. Then the darting team would approach and shoot a dart filled with drugs to bring the animal down. It takes about ten to thirty minutes for an elephant to go down. It takes us another thirty to forty minutes to fit the collar and take several measurements and notes on the physical attributes of the elephant. Then an antidote to the drug is administered through the veins in the ear of the elephant and the animal is usually up in five to ten minutes and ready to wander off. There are several variables that are not under our control and that meant we would have to be extra careful and prepared for all eventualities.

As we packed two radio collars, two receivers and a bunch of tools into the Gypsy, our trusted Suzuki four-wheel drive vehicle, I dwelled on how the project seemed to be taking a whole new direction with this crop-raiding bull. Time would eventually prove, however, that AJT's decision was one of the best for the project.

Reaching Motichur on the ninth of December 1995, we dropped our luggage at the forest rest house and left to do a quick reconnaissance of the area where the elephant bull was said to be roaming. This was to be my first collaring operation and I wanted to do my homework thoroughly. I spent the evening inspecting the damage he had caused.

The western part of Rajaji was separated from the eastern part by the river Ganges. The only connection between the two sides is provided by a narrow corridor between Motichur rau, one of the numerous seasonally dry river courses, and the Song river on the western bank of Ganges. The bull was operating in this narrow corridor area on the western bank. This area was occupied by an army cantonment, villages, and fertile crop fields and was devoid of any forest except for a small patch of trees along the banks of Motichur rau, which only held water during the monsoon and was now a dry bed of boulders. The Song, on the other hand, was a perennial river. A road and a rail track connecting Haridwar in the west and Rishikesh in the east, two of India's holiest towns, also bisected the corridor. The noise from the traffic in the corridor area was constant and loud. It took a very brave elephant (or a deaf one) to be using this area at all.

The forest guard told me that this particular tusker was very large and a regular winter visitor. The bull conducted his precision raids during the night and spent the daytime sleeping in the thick forests of Rajaji, just across the road. He seemed to know the area well and usually headed straight for his target crop fields or houses with harvested crop.

The previous night he had raided a village called Kandgaon near the army cantonment. We headed there and were greeted by a crowd of people all trying to speak at the same time. The general consensus seemed to be that it was a 'Bahut bada haathi', i.e. a very big elephant. From the tracks on the ground I could see that the raider was indeed a big elephant. With my less than superlative command of Hindi, it took a while before we could figure out whose household exactly he had raided the previous night. The main protagonist, Ramprasad, was identified and he proceeded to narrate the event to us. Ramprasad's wife and children had been sleeping inside their mud and thatch hut, while he himself slept out on a charpoy under a raised wooden platform in the front. The maize cobs they had harvested two days previously had been laid out on the platform to keep them dry and safe from cattle and goats. They hadn't bargained on an elephant.

Around midnight, Ramprasad was rudely roused from sleep by a deluge of maize cobs, exposing the folly of sleeping under such tasty and attractive food for elephants. In front of him were two massive black columns, otherwise known as elephant legs. The bull had simply pulled at one of the bamboo poles holding up the platform and sent the cobs raining down. He then proceeded to snack on them one by one, in front of the affronted owner, without so much as a by-your-leave.

Occasionally, when death stares a man in his face, he is prompted to think clearly. Ramprasad crawled out from the opposite side of the half-collapsed platform and shouted to his wife.

Awakened by the shouts, she picked up the infant sleeping with her and ran out, shouting, and straight into the elephant in her front yard. Evidently, the bull did not think much of this, because he ignored her and continued eating.

Ramprasad's shouts had roused people from nearby huts and they rushed to help their neighbour. They yelled as loud as they could in the hope of scaring the elephant away. For some reason, yelling tends to annoy most elephants. This bull was no exception. He took a few steps in the direction of the noise. In an instant, both the neighbours and their neighbourly concern had vanished and the bull went back to munching on his corn.

Ramprasad's three older children who had been sleeping in another room of the hut were now awake. The eldest son peeped out and saw a massive elephant, with white tusks, standing in their courtyard, feeding on their hard-earned harvest. Frightened out of their wits, the young children screamed for their parents.

This time, the unwelcome guest became seriously irritated. He walked to the hut and pushed the wall with his forehead. Mercifully, the hut, made of mud and sticks, didn't collapse and the children at once subsided into frightened sobs and whimpers. He again turned his attention to the maize. At one point, reaching for more of the corn, the elephant stepped on Ramprasad's overturned charpoy which promptly broke in two. The bull simply picked it up and tossed it aside.

Meanwhile, the neighbours felt obliged to return. Someone had turned up with a fire torch, and a few more torches were hastily assembled. Ramprasad, along with a few brave men of the village, advanced on the bull. Seeing the line of humans carrying fire made the elephant uneasy and he retreated to the forest along the rail track.

After an hour's detailed post-mortem of the exciting incident, the villagers dispersed to their respective huts and houses to catch up on their interrupted sleep. Ramprasad's wife and children went to sleep in the still-intact room while he sat outside with a log fire.

Half an hour later, just as he was beginning to nod off, Ramprasad sensed he was being watched. Looking up, he saw the incorrigible bull elephant had returned and was standing still at the edge of the circle of light thrown by the small log fire. Ramprasad grabbed the log and jumped up, waving it in front of the elephant and shouting for help at the same time. The hapless villagers again tumbled out of their huts and created another din.

The bull seemed to take in the situation. Then, having contemplated his options, thought better of it and ambled off to the forest. What they didn't know was that after he had walked off, he went into the cantonment area. There he broke a guard's tent and fed on a *Mallotus* shrub for more than an hour. That morning he had been seen near the army butchery walking towards the forest across the road. A forest guard and a soldier, deputed by the army to protect nearby villages from this elephant, had seen him and fired a few shots over his head. The bull made off at quite a pace at that point, and finally disappeared, but not before he ate some sugarcane from the village headman's field as a parting shot.

The villagers were naturally very agitated as they narrated the story to me. They wanted something done. I promised them that we would collar the trespasser and though they didn't understand what this meant, they knew somebody was at last taking action. The assurance helped to calm them down somewhat.

I asked Ramprasad, 'Did you notice if the elephant was in *musth* or limping from an injury?' Ramprasad replied, 'Nahin Sir, *lekin is haathi ka daina danth thoda toota hai.*' (No Sir, but its right tusk is a little broken.)

We decided to return early the next day to pick up his tracks. Back at the rest house, my mind was a whirlpool of thoughts as I tried to digest the information I had gleaned from a few hours in the field. It was lucky that no one got hurt in the raids by this bull. At the same time, I couldn't help but be amused by his antics. He was quite the rascal. I was amazed at the boldness he exhibited in raiding crops among the villages. Two or three decades ago, these areas would have been part of his forest home. I admired him for his stubbornness in refusing to let humans push him out of what he rightfully considered his turf.

Thus was born his name, Tipu, after the legendary Tipu Sultan, ruler of Mysore in eighteenth-century south India who refused to bow before the might of the British during their rule of India, and died in battle defending his kingdom.

Meanwhile, AJT, along with Dr. Pradip Malik, the Institute's wildlife veterinarian, and Dr. Surendra Goyal, one of my faculty supervisors from the Institute, had reached the Motichur forest rest house for the collaring operations next day. They were joined by my good friend Yashveer, a senior research fellow who had worked on ibex in the remote mountains of Himachal Pradesh.

The two captive elephants owned by the Park, Premkali and Arundhati, had also arrived from another camp to Motichur. Wild elephants are easiest to approach on the back of a captive elephant for darting and also the safest way to approach the darted elephant. Thus in most collaring operations, where trained captive elephants are available and the terrain is not too steep, using them was the preferred option.

I briefly told them about what I had heard and seen that evening and was sure that it wouldn't be difficult to track Tipu. Dr. Malik asked me, 'How big do you think the bull is judging from its tracks?'

'Around ten feet tall,' I replied. In Asian elephants, twice the circumference of the front foot is roughly the shoulder height of the elephant.

While this conversation was going on, AJT, Dr. Malik and Yashveer were sipping some foreign whiskey. I made do with the fried fish that they had brought along, all the while looking longingly at the bottle. Since I was expected to go out tracking before dawn, I wasn't offered a drink. Later Yashveer managed to smuggle in a glass of whiskey to the room we shared for the night.

The next morning, I left at 4.30 a.m. with Ram Sharan and Meghraj to pick up Tipu's tracks. The plan was I would leave the two of them there and come back to get the others. Govind, our driver would take us.

It was dark and cold and I saw early morning mists rising from the waters of the Song river. I was confident that Tipu would raid one of the villages and it would be an easy job tracking him from there.

My confidence was misplaced. Tipu did not make any village visits that night. Dejected at our failure to locate him, I went back to the Motichur Rest House.

The others were sipping their morning tea and awaiting news about Tipu's whereabouts. My report brought disappointment. AJT, however, was philosophical and said, 'Where can the elephant go? He will raid tomorrow or maybe day after tomorrow! We will wait and take him.'

A short while later, the Forest Range Officer of Motichur, Mr. J.T. Varma, came to tell us that he had sent all his staff out on patrols to the villages on the other side of the Song river to see if they could pick up Tipu's tracks.

As we sat around waiting for news of the pachyderm to arrive, I was feeling quite anxious to get going. Never having participated in a collaring operation before and having heard stories of things going horribly wrong in previous collaring efforts in Rajaji and elsewhere, I wanted to get the first one out of the way soon. We were having lunch when one of the forest staff came with news that had come over the wireless about an elephant having raided a village named Chiddarwalla on the other side of the Song river. A quick discussion later, the decision was made to proceed to the village in our vehicles and try our luck, opportunity permitting, on foot.

Dr. Malik was not enthusiastic about darting Tipu without the help of the trained captive elephants of Rajaji. AJT had decided we must go without the elephants since the village was too far away to move the elephants quickly enough. We loaded both the Gypsies with the equipment and headed for the village, guided by a Forest Department staff member.

At the village, largely inhabited by Nepali-speaking people, an elderly gentleman volunteered to take us to the house that had been raided. We set off in single file on a narrow path between fields cultivated with sugarcane, maize and paddy.

Soon, we came to a muddy road running along a stream that formed the boundary between the forest and the village. About 200 metres along the road, we came upon a fresh dung pile. One look at the undigested maize in it and I was sure it came from the by-now-infamous corn-snacker, Tipu.

We reached the house, a strong brick-and-cement-mortar structure. However, the kitchen, which had received Tipu's unwanted attention, was behind the house and made of thatch and mud.

It was incredible that any elephant could have raided it the way he had. To reach it, he had to squeeze through a narrow path between the main house and another hut nearby, both of which were untouched. He had stood in this passage, knocked down the top portion of the kitchen mud wall facing him and, in the dark, had investigated with his trunk for things to eat. He had pulled out a bag with wheat flour and consumed it, along with some salt kept in a plastic packet.

The people in the house had shouted and raised an alarm, but it had no effect on him. He left when he was ready to, only after finding nothing else to eat.

All this was being narrated with a great deal of emotion by the occupants of the house, and I could see AJT's eye twinkling with laughter. I tried to keep as straight a face as possible, but clearly it was an impossible task and the realization came to me that despite his blatant thieving, we were dealing with an eminently likeable elephant. By then, it was already late in the evening and the others had to leave for Dehradun, but they promised to return the next day, while I was tasked with tracking down Tipu.

The next morning, I moved to the forest rest house at Satyanarayan. Premkali and Arundhati, the captive elephants, also moved along with us to the new location. This location, near Song river, was closer to the villages Tipu was raiding. That evening, I heard a very interesting story from a local 'friend' of Tipu's.

Raju, an eccentric character who lived in a ramshackle structure made up of plywood boards haphazardly assembled under the railway overbridge near Raiwala, made his living by collecting the sugarcane that fell from the trucks passing under the bridge and selling it to small vegetable and fruit vendors. Making a living in Raju's world meant earning enough to buy a bottle of the locally-brewed liquor.

Ever since Tipu started plaguing the villages, Raju had taken to placing a heap of sugarcane in front of his hovel in the belief that his house would not be damaged if he made that offering every day. It seemed to work, because Tipu regularly came from the forest area along the rail track, climbed down near the overbridge, ate the pile of sugarcane and then went on his way to the village below. He ignored the fire and the smelly alcohol a few metres away that, together, served to keep Raju warm.

Raju sincerely believed that Tipu was his friend and invited us to come and spend the night with him near the fire. We sent him on his way after I agreed to visit him in the hope that he would be able to show me Tipu.

That night, we went looking for Raju. As described by Raju, there was a smouldering fire, a pile of sugarcane and large elephant tracks running along the side of his hovel. Of Raju, however, there was no sign. We waited around the fire in the hope Tipu would appear. Around

1:30 a.m., seeing no sign of Tipu, we left to check on the two villages that had been raided often in the previous two weeks. Raju told me the next morning that he had drunk too much and gone to sleep earlier than usual. I had a sense that this particular friendship was based on a shared appreciation of fermented juice.

At the first village, Pratipnagar, we found the men standing around two or three large piles of dry bushes and shrubs, waiting to light them if Tipu appeared.

In one corner of the village, I noticed that somebody had kept some gur (sticky brown molasses), and lighted a little lamp next to it. On enquiring about this offering, I was told by a villager that Tipu was no ordinary elephant, but the Lord Ganesha himself. I told him that they were encouraging the elephant to come every day by putting out such goodies. They looked at me with the type of pity the believer reserves for the infidel.

The women and children of the village had been moved to another nearby, smaller village to protect them from Tipu. Reassuring them that we would surely do something about him, we went to the next village of Kandgaon.

Unlike in Pratipnagar, here there were no big fires. Small fires danced in a couple of places and the whole village appeared to be sleeping. The reason, I opined loudly, was probably because most houses here were made of concrete. Even the few villagers, like Ramprasad, with mud houses, had no more reason to worry, for Tipu had wiped out almost his entire winter harvest of maize. Ramprasad was sleeping peacefully when I went to check his hut.

Around 2:30 a.m., when sleep finally overtook us, we returned to the rest house for a nap. A few hours later, I woke with a start and realized that I was shivering in spite of the blanket. It was still dark, and a glance at my watch indicated it was 5:50 a.m. I woke Ram Sharan and asked him to make some tea and wake the others. We had steaming cups of tea and then went back to Pratipnagar.

The sight that greeted me was shocking. Two of the huts near the firewood pile had their roofs pulled off. The walls appeared as if some giant fist had smashed them in. We had scarcely parked, when people poured out of the huts and alleys and surrounded the Gypsy. They were very agitated and, even with my rudimentary understanding of the language, I gathered they were telling me in no uncertain terms that we were just like the Indian police in Bollywood movies—always arriving at the crime scene after the robbers had fled.

Someone from the back of the crowd shouted, '*Chalo inki gaari jala dete hai*' which means 'Let us burn their vehicle'. I had never faced an angry mob like this in my previous life in south India, and was quite taken aback and more than a bit apprehensive, but managed to keep my fear under control.

On spying a young man who seemed to be slightly less agitated than the others, I pulled him aside and asked him to tell me exactly what had happened. He said that after we had left, as dawn approached, everyone let their guard down. Most returned to their huts to catch a few winks. The fires started to go out. Tipu had crossed the canal running on one side of the village and come up behind the few people who were still around the dying fires. He had walked in the shadows and eaten the gur offering they had left and then walked towards the hut. One of the villagers suddenly realized that the bull was in the village and raised an alarm.

Tipu, by now quite experienced, charged them and cleared his immediate surrounding of people. He then turned around and walked towards the huts, which were on either side of a footpath and pulled the bamboo poles supporting the roof of one. The roof came off in an instant. He wasn't bothered about the fire that had, by then, died down to embers. In fact, he left a big elephant pad mark on the ashes, as if to indicate what he thought of it.

Years of raiding practice meant that he knew exactly where the uncrushed wheat and flour were stored. He pulled out a bag of flour from the first hut and ate it. After finishing the flour, he knocked the wall down and checked for other things to eat, feeling around with his trunk. On finding nothing, he moved to the next hut and repeated the roof pulling. Not finding anything to eat there, he then proceeded to knock down the wall.

Here, he encountered a sewing machine given to the lady of the house by the government. He tossed it down and it broke. Then, he put an end to the lady's tailoring dreams by stepping on it. He rewarded himself for all the effort with a small bag of wheat he found during his rummaging.

All the while, the villagers kept shouting and banging things to make noise. The young man told me that they were afraid of irritating him more. At around 5:30 a.m., he walked along a path that ran under the railway tracks, crossed the river and was now somewhere in the forest on the Park side of the main road.

I instructed one of the assistants to fetch Premkali to follow him. It now seemed our decision to move the captive elephants and their mahouts along with the associated staff closer to the action was a good idea. The mahouts and the assistant mahouts are invaluable to the collaring effort. The captive elephants listen only to their commands and the mahouts understand wild elephant behaviour because of the close bonds they form with their own elephants. An important point to note is that the Asian elephant is probably the only animal that has been in captivity for more than 4,000 years and has not been domesticated and bred into various forms of elephants like other livestock that humans took from the wild like chicken, cattle and dogs.

Ram Sharan informed that the captive elephants were being readied and he also heard that Habib, Premkali's assistant mahout, had seen Tipu cross the road near the all-night tea shop along the main road while he was having his morning cup of tea. By then, the collaring team had arrived minus Yashveer. I updated them on the latest information about Tipu's whereabouts, and Dr. Malik quickly prepared a dart, loaded the rifle and handed it to AJT.

In another 15 minutes, Premkali arrived at the tea shop. AJT, along with two forest guards, climbed on Premkali and the mahout gave the command for her to enter the jungle. The rest of us followed on foot with the equipment and antidote.

Dr. Malik had fallen off the back of a captive elephant during a collaring operation in North Bengal the previous month, where he had been caught in the middle of a wild elephant group and had had a miraculous escape. Still shaken at the experience, he decided to stay with the vehicles and be in contact with us over the wireless radio.

The area was filled with lantana bushes, and once we entered it, I realized that we were helpless since nothing was visible beyond Premkali's ample backside. We couldn't see more than a few feet in front of us and there was little light penetrating from above. The thorny lantana stems added to the precarious situation by tugging and tearing our skin and clothes. If we came face to face with Tipu in these bushes, I knew we were doomed.

After fifteen minutes, we lost track of the darting team atop Premkali and were totally disoriented. Now and then, we would run into women collecting fodder or firewood and they would tell us the direction in which Premkali had gone.

AJT and Motilal, a colourful character from the Forest Department experienced in collaring operations, were also having a difficult time finding their way. They were dependent on the guard from the local forest office who was mortally afraid of Tipu. I suspect he didn't want to go near Tipu, so he misled the people on Premkali saying he knew where the elephant usually rested and led them away from where he thought Tipu might actually be.

After half an hour of wandering aimlessly, they discovered that he didn't know what he was talking about and also had no idea where they were in the forest. A quick elephant-top conference later, Motilal and AJT decided that they would come back to the main road and try picking up Tipu's tracks from the road using our assistants Meghraj and Ram Sharan.

Meanwhile, our group started shouting to indicate our location and were met within minutes by Premkali and her riders. Together, we stumbled back to the road for another attempt.

Ram Sharan and Meghraj, along with Habib, then picked up the tracks from near the tea shop from where Tipu was last seen going into the jungle, and the rest of us followed them with Premkali behind us.

The tracking was difficult, but with years of experience in following elephants, the assistants kept their eyes to the ground and kept going.

Occasionally, they would lose the tracks and then scout in different directions in a circular manner, while the rest of us tried to stay out of their path to avoid confusing them. Then there would be a celebratory shout and we would set off again.

The weather was cold and the sun had just begun shining when we reached the point where the tracks crossed a stream. Picking up the tracks on the other side of the stream, we walked into thick lantana. The tracks seemed to be fresh, and along the track were broken and bent stems and seedlings.

AJT called a halt for a quick consultation, after which it was decided that the darting team would get on Premkali while the rest of us would follow her closely.

Dr. Goyal followed the darting team on foot as he was carrying the large animal and human antidote, essential components of a darting operation used to revive the tranquillized animal or a human darted accidentally. It is important to revive a darted elephant immediately in cases where it falls into an awkward position or on its sternum, both of which could end up killing it. Generally, an elephant should not be left lying on its chest and belly, also called sternal recumbency, for more than ten to fifteen minutes. In this position, the intestines in their large bellies filled with food, exert great pressure on the diaphragm. This, in turn, inhibits normal breathing and, if not revived within a few minutes, will result in the death of the darted elephant.

We must have proceeded for a few minutes when Motilal gave a low whistle to indicate that the bull was in sight. Premkali came to a halt and refused to move forward. I knew that Johor, Premkali's primary mahout, was afraid of Tipu and she had sensed his fear. I told AJT that it would be better for fearless Habib, the assistant mahout, to be in command of Premkali at that point.

Places were duly swapped and it was amazing to see the change that came over the elephant. Premkali immediately started moving towards Tipu at Habib's command, delivered as a signal with his feet behind her ears. It also indicated the close bond mahouts form with their elephants—the elephants can sense the mood of their mahouts and respond to it.

The rest of the team, including the trackers, moved off diagonally to a safe distance. To get a good view and watch the action, I climbed a thin tree and settled myself on a branch about fifteen feet above the ground.

Tipu was huge and it was then that I noticed he was in full musth, with his temporal glands open and the sticky fluid streaming down the sides of his face. Some of it dribbled into his mouth. Musth is a condition where males experience heightened levels of testosterone and is equivalent to the rut in deer. This is a period where the elephant bull is only interested in searching for females in heat to mate with them, though elephants can also mate with females outside their musth period. Elephants in musth are usually very aggressive and non-musth males give them a wide berth. Usually males have to be in good health before they will come into musth. Tipu looked really fat. Not a single bone was visible.

As soon as he heard Premkali moving towards him in the lantana, he whirled around to face her. When the darting team on Premkali saw him turn and take a couple of steps in their direction, they moved away hastily.

Suddenly, I found myself alone in the audience, on my treetop seat, in a theatre where the cast on stage before me had vanished. To add insult to abandonment, they had taken both the darting rifle and the shotgun. I had been very eager to see Tipu, but now I wasn't so sure. Tipu was over ten feet tall and here I was, a thin researcher on a thin branch, very much within his reach if he should decide to stretch his trunk in my direction.

From my vantage point atop it, the tree which was a tree when I climbed it, suddenly felt like a forlorn stick stuck in the ground. To say that I felt vulnerable would be a ludicrous understatement.

My heart pounded fast and my palms became sticky with sweat. The fear beat in deafening pulses in my head and I was convinced that there was no way Tipu couldn't hear it even though he was some distance away.

After a couple of minutes, he turned around and moved away. Just then, Premkali re-appeared and then disappeared again, this time behind Tipu into the thick lantana bushes.

Some ten minutes of nervous waiting later, I heard the dart gun go off, followed by shouting. I jumped down from the tree and met the assistants and Dr. Goyal coming towards me. We homed in on the noise to find Premkali calmly feeding on some twigs and the darting team in animated conversation. There was no sign of Tipu.

The dart had missed, passing over its target in a futile arc. AJT was having trouble ejecting the spent cartridge from the rifle. Luckily, the Institute had assigned Vinod, a technician in charge of keeping all equipment in working condition, to the collaring operation. He had the presence of mind to fashion a spent cartridge ejector from a key ring and eject the empty cartridge. The rifle was reloaded with a new cartridge and the spare dart and the tracking resumed.

Tipu hadn't moved far since the previous encounter, and after a few minutes, the gun went off again. When the dart hit him squarely on the side, he took three or four quick steps in retreat, then slowed to his regular pace. There was no sign of fear or any reaction from being injected with a powerful narcotic drug, a drop of which is sufficient to kill an adult human being within minutes if it touches broken skin.

Tipu was busy feeding and displayed no intention whatsoever of going under sedation. Soon he started moving and reached within sight of the railway tracks running through the forest. For lack of a better idea, we followed.

Somebody had the good sense to send Ram Sharan to fetch another freshly prepared dart from Dr. Malik stationed near the tea shop, about a kilometre away. All of us were now at the railway track, about fifty metres from Tipu, waiting impatiently for Ram Sharan to return. A train went past at breakneck speed, but neither the noise nor the sight of a speeding train had any effect on Tipu. Soon, he stood still and we thought that the drug was finally taking effect. Wrong!

After about thirty minutes, Tipu walked leisurely to a muddy waterhole nearby and started to spray water and throw mud on himself. AJT, who had decided that his darting prowess had been mocked enough, wasted no time in loading the dart gun when Ram Sharan returned with the spare dart. He approached Tipu along the railway line and shot him on the left shoulder. Tipu again took three or four quick strides back into the lantana, then went still.

By then, the other captive elephant, Arundhati, had arrived and we climbed on the two elephants to keep Tipu in sight. We waited for him to fall any moment. Instead, twenty minutes later, the incorrigible elephant started feeding again.

We were at our wit's end. AJT called me over, handed me the gun and asked me to have it loaded with another dart. I dismounted, waded into a stream and reached the railway track all wet and muddy to find Dr. Malik waiting there. He immediately vetoed any more darting for the day.

I had to agree with Dr. Malik's decision. We hadn't propitiated the gods right. Tipu seemed to be impervious to any kind of chemical immobilization. We packed up and decided to try our luck afresh the next morning.

That night, many theories floated over glasses of whiskey as to why the darts had no effect on the elephant. It was all wild conjecture. None of the theories made any sense. Dr. Malik assured me, 'Don't worry, I will make sure that your study animals are collared.' And on that note, we all stumbled into bed and fell sound asleep.

The next morning, we set out at 5 a.m. After having been chastened by the angry mob the previous morning we decided to give Pratipnagar a wide berth and headed straight to the roadside tea shop to enquire about our recalcitrant quarry.

Fortunately, the cook at the tea shop had seen Tipu cross the road about fifteen minutes earlier. We immediately sent word over the wireless to wake up the main team and get the camp elephants ready. By 7:30 a.m., everyone had gathered at the tea shop.

This time, it was the darting team on Premkali, led by Ram Sharan and Meghraj, that set off into the forest to trace Tipu. Dr. Goyal and I, along with a couple of others, climbed up on gentle Arundhati's back with the collars and related paraphernalia and followed.

We must have been moving for about fifteen to twenty minutes when Motilal whistled to alert our mahout. Ahead was Tipu, towering over the lantana bushes and looking in the direction of Premkali, flummoxed by this persistent lady admirer. In the elephant world, it is the convention for males to follow females. The legend of Cupid not being common knowledge among elephants, he wasn't sure what the darts were, but he seemed to know that Premkali and the strange humans atop her had something to do with the pinpricks he had been subjected to the previous day.

I leaned over and whispered to our mahout to lead Arundhati around and behind Tipu so we could distract him and give the darting team a chance to approach him. We moved directly behind him and I borrowed the mahout's machete and banged it against a tree trunk. While I was quite pleased with the sound generated, Tipu was unimpressed and did not even bother to look around.

Premkali was made to move in an arc around Tipu so AJT could attempt a shoulder shot. Tipu followed Premkali's move and turned to faced her head on again. There was no shoulder target to aim at. Premkali was dwarfed by this giant of an elephant. And though I continued to bang the machete, it did not distract him in the least. Then, suddenly, he turned to move away and AJT got his shot. Tipu rushed into the bushes.

Signs from the darting team on Premkali indicated a successful hit. Within five minutes, Premkali and Arundhati tracked him down. He was standing a short distance away. As time ticked by, there was no sign that the drug had started to take effect. In about fifteen minutes, however, he started swaying. In another five minutes, Tipu simply sat down on his hind quarters, slid onto his side, and passed out.

The drug had finally worked! We approached him as quietly as possible. He waved his trunk feebly a couple of times and then lay completely still. Someone picked up a stick and prodded him. When there was no response, we climbed down in a jiffy and got to work collaring him.

He was truly a big elephant. We measured his shoulder height and even with his forelegs slightly bent, he was over ten and a half feet tall. Till today, he remains the tallest elephant recorded in Rajaji National Park. Dr. Goyal kept a careful eye on his breathing. Tipu inhaled. (A breathing cycle in elephants can be up to a minute as the air makes its way up that long trunk and back out.) Just then, Govind, our adventurous young driver, approached Tipu with a swagger and tried to lift his trunk. He had succeeded in lifting the tip of the trunk a centimetre or two when Tipu exhaled and the air came rushing out into Govind's face.

The look on Govind's face changed to pure terror. He thought the elephant had woken and in his panic, dropped the trunk, jumped backwards, tripped and fell head over heels, and scrambled away on all fours into the lantana. Much laughter ensued and Govind never quite lived that down in the next four years as project driver.

Meanwhile, Tipu had fallen onto the root of a nearby tree and we struggled to dig under his neck to get the collar through. Time was running out and I dug madly from one side while Ram Sharan, hidden by Tipu's massive body, dug from the other. Finally, after some frantic digging, I lay flat on the ground with my entire right arm under Tipu's neck in what seemed like an awkward moment of drunken brotherly camaraderie. In the mud I felt one edge of the collar that Ram Sharan was pushing come through. Relieved, we quickly slipped the collar around Tipu's neck and tightened the nuts and bolts.

While the others were busy cutting the extra length of the collar, I took my first opportunity to take a good look at Tipu. He was a handsome tusker with not a bone visible under the fat. The pads on his feet, which must have seen many miles, were covered with cracks all over.

His forehead was sunken, indicating his more advanced age. His left temporal gland was open and reddish, with sticky fluid streaming from it. This secretion has a strong smell and you can smell an elephant two or three hours after he has passed that way. He was just coming into musth that male elephants in their prime come into every year for a few months.

After I had given Tipu and his new collar a final once-over, Dr. Goyal gave him an antidote. We climbed onto the backs of Premkali and Arundhati and moved some distance away, leaving AJT to sit in a tree nearby to photograph Tipu reviving.

Within five minutes, AJT saw Tipu sit up, then stand and finally walk away with the tranquillizer dart still stuck to his left rump. He had fallen on his left side and it had been impossible for us to reach it when he went down. We all heaved a sigh of relief as he moved away, and headed back to the rest house for a much needed breakfast.

It so happened that with the onset of musth, Tipu left the corridor area and went into the Park in search of females. The crop and house-raiding stopped completely. Tracking him over the next few days, I found him in the happy company of oestrus (ovulating) females who were in the mood to mate with him.

With his musth-related disappearance coinciding with our operation, I became quite a hero in the areas where he had been crop-raiding. Random strangers would stop to talk to us and offer to buy us tea while we were in the Raiwala area where Tipu had been collared. They would congratulate me on a job well done and I would whisper advice to Ram Sharan and Govind to make hay while the sun shone, because these very same people would be baying for our blood come next winter when the incorrigible Tipu returned to resume crop-raiding, which he did.

While it is a serious matter to have a five-tonne elephant knocking down one's walls and eating one's crops, Tipu, by virtue of the force of his personality, became quite a legend during the time we tracked him. He provided me with many valuable insights into elephant behaviour. Above all, I learnt that while being the biggest and bravest, he was a gentle giant who, despite living in close proximity to thousands of people, never harmed anyone. To us, he was the gentle giant of the Siwaliks.

CHAPTER 4

Collaring and Tracking Elephants

At the end of 1996, after collaring and tracking Tipu for a few days, I came back to the Institute and found a letter from my mother informing me that my grandfather had passed away. Having lost my father, who had been more a friend than a father, a year before, and then losing my grandfather, the one person who believed in me the most, was a double whammy. I needed to go home.

I took leave for a month. India was then still the land of long-distance trunk calls and telegrams. Flying was a luxury that very few could afford. It took a student, living on a research fellowship like myself four days by train and bus to reach my home in Coonoor, near Ootacamund in south India.

While I was away, AJT led the elephant collaring team to complete three more successful captures—two females and another male. I regretted having missed out on the action, but was happy to return to a decent count of collared elephants for my study.

The male, who was about thirty-five to forty years of age, had only his right tusk. My field assistants named him Shahrukh, after India's reigning Bollywood hero, mostly because his collaring had entailed quite a bit of drama. He had been darted in the evening and had promptly disappeared into thick shrubs where the team lost his tracks. Several groups attempted to track him down, but failed. As the evening light started to fade, the search became one tinged with desperation.

On a whim, Ram Sharan and Yasin decided to pick up the search on the dry rau bed that ran along the edge of the forest patch where he had been darted. To their relief, they found him collapsed on his chest on the rau bed, near the roots of a ficus. Nearly an hour had gone by since he was darted. Fortunately, he fell with one of his rear legs tucked under him, and that had kept his chest off the ground.

A quick discussion had ensued, with the team deciding to revive him immediately. Dr. Goyal insisted that the collar be put on him posthaste, which they did before reviving him just as the remaining light disappeared. There had been no time to cut the excess length of the belt, so Shahrukh walked around for the next two years with a piece of collar belt hanging below his neck, much like a jaunty film star's neckerchief.

Shahrukh was, for the most part, a mild-tempered elephant. Understandable, given that he was slightly on the smaller side for his age. He tended to avoid humans and fights with other elephants. When he came into musth, however, he displayed a total change in personality. His aggression was particularly focused on vehicles, and he would temporarily take to charging any offending four-wheeler within sight.

The older of the two collared females lived in a close-knit group with two other adult females and their offspring. She was very beautiful, with noticeably long eyelashes. I named her Mallika, after India's famous danseuse Mallika Sarabhai who was known for her beautiful eyes and long lashes.

She had a juvenile daughter, Malavika, and an older son. He was about four or five years old and had distinctive divergent tusks, so I just referred to him as DivT. What I didn't know was that Mallika was pregnant again.

The younger collared female we named Aishwarya, after Aishwarya Rai, the stunning

Indian beauty queen who had just won the Miss World title two years before. We could hardly be blamed for the naming process, as we were all bachelors (the driver, field assistants and myself) and the closest we came to famous and beautiful women in those years was when we were tracking these elephant ladies. We found that Aishwarya lived in a very unstable group. One day, I would count thirty elephants, and on other days, I would only see Aishwarya and her juvenile daughter with a couple of much older elephants and their calves.

Collaring elephants in a forested habitat is never easy and definitely not fun when you are in the middle of it. A hundred things can go wrong, but we had managed to collar a total of four elephants without any major mishap.

Unlike in the African savannah where elephants are located and darted from helicopters, making it a relatively easy operation, one is totally dependent on captive elephants in the tropical forests of Asia. In places where trained captive elephants are not available, all darting must be done on foot—an incredibly dangerous undertaking.

It is only when the dart hits the elephant that the drama really starts to unfold. Sometimes when the drug acts slowly, the darted elephants can run two to three kilometres before collapsing. During the chaos, the tracking team can't afford to lose their quarry. It also happens that if they are in a group, the group will run in one direction and the darted elephant, as the drug starts acting, gets disorientated and makes off in a different direction. At least on one occasion, we have ended up chasing the wrong elephant and lost valuable time. There is also the ever-present danger of sternal recumbency, as happened to Shahrukh.

There were enough horror stories from other research studies about elephants dying during tranquillizing operations to wake me in a cold sweat the night before every collaring operation. The most important lesson was that one had to assume that things might go wrong at any given point and prepare for it rather than winging it during a crisis. The first-hand lessons I learnt about darting and collaring elephants in Rajaji stood me in good stead in later years during elephant collaring operations in Borneo and Sumatra.

With four collared elephants to track and collect data from, I soon found myself very busy running around the park locating them. I was still new to radio tracking and it took a while before I could locate the elephants efficiently. The assistants were more experienced, having already followed two other collared elephants on the eastern bank of the Ganges in previous years. They were key in helping me track the elephants.

I was learning how to approach elephants without disturbing them so I could observe their feeding habits and behaviour. This was more easily said than done, given that they had such a sharp sense of smell, and the slightest change in wind direction would alert them to my presence.

It was nerve-racking to be in thick undergrowth, hearing elephant sounds all around but not being able to see them.

One day, Ram Sharan and I climbed a hill in the Beribada area in search of Tipu. We located him, still in musth, standing on a hillside overlooking a steep wooded valley. We had approached him from above, so assuming we were safe, we sat down to watch. Tipu saw us approaching and cocked his head to look at us for some time. Then he turned away and stood looking intently down into the valley. This puzzled me. Elephants usually do not turn away from a potential threat unless they are running or intending to move away. Below Tipu was a steep animal trail running down to the valley. Except for the occasional birdcall, the valley itself was very quiet.

Suddenly, silence was broken by a deep elephant rumble from the bottom of the valley, followed by a high-pitched trumpet that had protest written all over it. We heard it again. Immediately, Tipu moved to the edge of the hillside and called back in a rumble much deeper than anything I had heard before or since. In fact, not only did I hear his rumble, I felt its vibration in every pore of my body.

He was answered by another high-pitched protest trumpet. Within a couple of minutes, we saw a female with very long tushes coming up the hill along the trail. Tushes are thin incisors, which are basically underdeveloped tusks in females and some tuskless males. Close behind her followed an amorous young adult male, trying to hold her back with his trunk on her back, eager to mount her. Her protestations reverberated in the valley as she hurried up the trail.

Her calf followed them. Further behind, a procession of other elephants from the group came into view, browsing on Bauhinia leaves, climbing unhurriedly up the trail towards where Tipu was standing. Tipu became visibly more interested and edgy as more trumpets, squeals and rumbles came up the valley. It was almost ten minutes before the female had negotiated the climb to the top.

When the female was about fifty metres from Tipu, she half ran with her calf towards him. The young bull sensed Tipu's presence and abruptly stopped on the path.

I wondered idly if he might retreat down the trail.

Instead, as Tipu took two determined strides down the path towards him, the young bull let out a trumpet of fear and dashed up the hillside straight at us. To say that was unexpected would be an understatement. We turned just as suddenly and scrambled up the hill to get out of his way.

He trampled across the spot where we had been lounging seconds before, and then slid down on his haunches to reach the trail curving around the other side of the hill, which was a safe distance from Tipu. He then ran along the trail over the ridge and, for the next two to three minutes, we heard him go slipping and sliding all the way down the hill, dislodging loose rocks and sending them crashing down to the valley below.

Among African elephants, I had read about oestrus females actively seeking protection from big males to avoid harassment by younger adult males, a behaviour termed as soliciting guarding. I had just been privy to a ringside view of how it worked in Asian elephants, followed by the berserk 'losing' party breaching the ring and heading for the audience!

I had been naïve to think that elephants would not leave the trail on a steep hill slope. I still couldn't believe how fast the young bull had run straight up the hill! We were even more amazed at the speed at which we got out of the way.

Watching elephants was something that I enjoyed immensely. However, seeing the elephants disturbed by the Gujjars was a constant source of irritation for me. I would spend hours tracking and locating the elephants, then spend close to an hour approaching them quietly, when suddenly some men and their buffaloes would descend loudly on the scene and cause the elephants to flee.

I found it odd that most of the tribespeople, even having lived in elephant forests for so long, displayed absolutely no sensitivity towards elephants. At the very sight of them they would start hollering and screaming. Most of the time this bedlam succeeded in chasing away elephants, especially the female groups and younger males. Occasionally, however, they would run into a bull in musth or a bull that just did not appreciate being hollered at. Then it would be their turn to run.

One day driving around a small bend on the forest road, we saw a big male in musth walking towards us. He looked calm and had the typical musth elephant swagger with his head held high and chin tucked in. We reversed the Gypsy some distance, while he stepped off the road and into the forest. We carried on down the road, and 200 metres ahead came upon a bicycle lying on the ground.

Fearing the worst, I got down to inspect the cycle when a tremulous voice called out from the heavens. I looked up and saw a Gujjar man clinging to a thin branch, some twenty-five feet above the ground. He was clearly terrified and refused to come back down to earth. It took me a while to convince him that the elephant had really left the scene.

He finally climbed down the tree and stood shaking. We sat him down and asked him what had transpired. It turned out that he had been cycling down the path without a care in the world, that is, until he cycled straight into the elephant's line of sight. The bull had been standing behind a tree, and as the man rattled into view, he just curled up his trunk and charged.

The man dropped his cycle posthaste and when the elephant paused in his charge to sniff it, he quickly climbed a nearby tree. That was where we had found him. In common parlance, it was what one could consider a narrow escape. Luckily, the bull left the cycle undamaged. So, after the man had calmed down somewhat, he got back on his cycle and went on his way.

I put this incident out of mind thinking it was a very rare one, but within a few weeks discovered that I was wrong. It became quite common for us to find cycles lying on the road, at which we would first laugh, then do a quick scan to see if it was one of our identified elephants until finally we would look up into the trees to find the cycle owners. Some of the more unflappable Gujjars would join us in the laughter after they climbed down.

It was not exactly easy for the tribe to be living in such close proximity to the elephants and having to go about the forests for their livelihood. One day, I found one of them holding a small child clinging onto some exposed roots on a steep, almost vertical, crumbling hillside along the rau while a bull in musth that had chased them up was standing at the foot of the hill. Ram Sharan and I clapped and shouted to distract him from the precarious situation into which he had placed the father and child. We succeeded because the bull then turned around and came straight for us in an unhurried manner. Behind him, the Gujjar climbed down and hurried away.

Every day, I learned something new about the Park, the elephants and the people living there. Field life settled into a nice pattern.

CHAPTER 5

Close Shaves

One afternoon, Ram Sharan and I were out tracking Shahrukh in a forest block that was used heavily by the people of the Gujjar tribe. Every available fodder tree there bore the telltale signs of lopping or cutting. The villagers usually lopped all branches within their reach for their buffaloes. Sometimes, the only green left would be on a few twigs at the top of the tree. The heavy lopping prevented the trees from producing seeds. The few seedlings that did manage to survive were more often than not trampled underfoot by the buffaloes.

Khair, a tree species called *Acacia catechu*, also happens to be a favourite food of elephants. The adult bulls, in order to reach the few remaining twigs on lopped trees, would push an entire tree down. It was the elephants, therefore, who took the blame for causing heavy damage to this tree species. From the Gujjars to veteran forest rangers, this belief was entrenched. It took me quite a while to understand that elephants were not the real cause of *Acacia catechu* decline in Rajaji.

Late in the afternoon, one day, we found Shahrukh in a plantation area of thorny Khair trees. He was partly hidden by some shrubs in the otherwise relatively open plantation area. He was about a hundred metres away from us as I watched his head bob up and down, indicating he was feeding on something.

Wanting to take a closer look, I left Ram Sharan behind and started to slowly approach the elephant. Using several termite mounds and the large leaves of teak saplings as cover, I edged closer to him. When I was about thirty metres away, I saw him feeding on the bark of lopped *Acacia* branches whose leaves had been eaten by the buffaloes. Shahrukh was methodically picking up each branch, rotating it in his mouth to remove the bark for consumption, then tossing aside the stripped branch before picking up another. So intent was I on watching him feed that I wasn't prepared for what happened next.

Before I realized that he had finished feeding under the tree, he quickly turned around and walked straight towards where I was sitting. Like an ostrich sticking its head in the ground in response to danger, I immediately ducked behind the nearest termite mound. The plantation area was so open, if I had got up to run, he would have seen me and not been happy about it.

Within a minute, I heard him feeding again. I peered from behind the termite mound and spied him under another *Acacia* tree, going through the same motions with the twigs under there. He was barely twenty metres away from me. I was completely underwhelmed by the lack of hiding places in this open plantation area. Deciding to do something about it, I gingerly crawled backwards on all fours hoping that he wouldn't notice me. I must have covered about five or six metres in reverse. As I reached a teak sapling with large leaves reaching almost to the ground, Shahrukh moved again in my direction. I quickly hid behind the curtain of teak leaves. The sapling itself was thinner than me, so that was ruled out as cover. Luckily for me, he was distracted by another *Acacia* tree just in time.

I looked around for an escape route, but all around was a sea of *Acacia* trees, with freshly-cut branches lying underneath. I started to panic and had to fight the urge to leap up and make a run for it. My imagination started playing tricks on me. I was quite convinced that Shahrukh was looking directly at me. Not only was he actually looking at me, he was walking towards me. Again.

In an inspired move, I quickly crawled to the other side of the termite mound and hunkered my six-foot frame into a blob about one foot high. Astoundingly, the forced humility worked. It felt surreal as I watched the elephant towering over me as he passed the termite mound three or four metres away. I became exceedingly calm (which, I believe, is known as catalepsy in medical terms).

Strangely though, it wasn't my entire life that flashed before my eyes, but rather the opposite. I saw the fine details of Shahrukh's great form, in slow motion. I saw the wrinkles in his leathery skin and the saliva-moistened tip of his trunk. I smelled the scent of freshly-crushed leaves and twigs from his mouth and heard the slap of his tail as he swatted flies.

The wind held. So did I. Shahrukh passed by unaware that he had committed a great kindness in sparing the life of a greenhorn wildlife biologist on the other side of that ridiculous termite mound. Especially kind, considering how few of us there are. When I judged him to be a safe enough distance away from me, I beat a hasty retreat in the opposite direction.

Perhaps it was not that much of a miracle that I escaped detection at such close quarters that day. It occurred to me that maybe just like humans, elephants also have a search image, i.e. you know what you are looking for and that item is what your brain will focus on even if given a choice of other items. That Wednesday it was *Acacia* branches for Shahrukh. Evidently, I didn't fit the description, though only by a whisker as I was also very thin and looked like a dry branch during those days. When I finally found Ram Sharan, I felt weak in the pit of my stomach but also extremely alive at the same time. I had never been so close to a wild elephant that was not knocked out silly by tranquillizers, and had been extremely foolish to not anticipate danger and extricate myself from the situation sooner. Thinking about how close I was to losing my life, I realized that nature was trying to teach me something. As an urbanized human, having lived in safe environments all my life, it was a wake-up call to sharpen my senses. Exhilarated by the encounter, it would still take a few more close shaves for me to realize that, if I wasn't careful, my luck would run out and people would start talking about me in the past tense.

A few days after the incident with Shahrukh, I set off early on a January dawn with the assistants to try and track Mallika. We detected her signal in one of the few undisturbed forest patches in Rajaji called Kania Nalla. The forest was still draped with a veil of winter mist and visibility was poor. Having a feeble signal, we decided to walk down a gentle meandering path running past several ficus trees to the nalla.

About a kilometre down, the trail took a sharp turn around a ficus. We rounded the bend and came face to face with a huge tusker. He was just a few strides away. The pungent smell of the musth-induced secretion hit my nostrils. Ram Sharan, Meghraj and I did an about-turn and bolted some distance down the path, then waited with the hope that he would walk off into the forest.

We must have waited for three or four minutes when the great grey beast materialized from the mist. He had not seen us, but, like a bloodhound following his prey, he had his trunk to the ground to track us. When I looked around, Ram Sharan and Meghraj, in a show of utter disloyalty, had disappeared. There is no other situation on earth that evokes the kind of fear you feel on being left to your own devices literally a few metres from a wild musth bull. (Later in life, I would realize that the nearest parallel might be when a perfectly chatty wife suddenly goes deadly silent.)

I leapt off the trail some distance into the forest, then looked back and paused. The bull had stopped and was intently smelling the place I had been standing at a few moments before. Then he seemed to make up his mind to follow because he, too, left the trail...exactly on my tracks. He was in full musth. I immediately half ran from that patch of forest and quickly doubled back to the trail, finally reaching the road from where we started earlier in the morning. There, I stopped to catch my breath and waited to see if Ram Sharan or Meghraj would reappear. Unbelievably, I saw the tusker loom like a ghost out of the white mist down the trail towards the road. I ran down the road towards our field camp. When I thought I had run a good distance, I stopped and looked back. There he was, determinedly coming down the road. He had been on my trail for over a kilometre now, like a confounded bloodhound, scaring the living daylights out of me. The hair on my arms stood on end.

As I neared the field camp, he stopped abruptly to smell the air, then veered off into the forest and disappeared from sight. As if on cue, Ram Sharan and Meghraj appeared out of the mist grinning widely and wondering where the tusker had gone. They even had the cheek to ask me why I had abandoned them.

As much as I used to be exasperated with the Gujjars for not looking out for elephants, I realized that we were no better when it came to being on the alert for danger. We had let our guard down that morning, walking down the path totally focused on locating Mallika and her family.

None of us had expected to be confronted by a bull. If he had been behind the ficus instead of a few strides away, as we turned around the bend, one of us would most certainly have been killed. It would have been the elephant that would then have been blamed. We had ignored one of the jungle's most elementary rules—at every turn, expect the unexpected.

Hardly a week later that January, I had another near-death experience that became the turning point in how we went about tracking elephants. That morning, while driving up a small rise in the road between two raus, I spied Vasanth, a handsome tusker about thirty years old, crossing the road. He was in musth and looked grand. For several weeks, I had been frustrated in my attempts to photograph him.

I grabbed the camera and jumped down from the Gypsy to get a shot of him, but he had already crossed the road and was heading to the rau. I caught sight of a trail nearby which, I mistakenly thought, ran parallel to the one he had taken, about thirty to forty metres apart.

I did a quick estimation and, aiming to get to the rau before he started crossing it, I ran down this parallel trail. When I reached the rau bank, there was a three-foot drop to the bed. Without thinking or looking out, I jumped down into the rau. I landed on my feet on the boulders and looked up to find Vasanth emerging into the rau hardly forty feet from me. My actions were too much of a provocation for a bull in musth. Without a single noise, he simply curled his trunk and charged.

I turned and jumped up the rau bank to retreat, but that morning there had been heavy dew, so I slipped on the wet leaves underfoot. As I fell, I twisted my body to keep my camera from hitting the ground. I fell hard on my back. The boulders rolled under his charging weight. The sound thundered in my ears. Less than ten feet away from me he paused, momentarily confused that I had disappeared from sight.

As I lay supine on the bank, I heard him blow loudly from his trunk, but it was the smell of his musth flow that overpowered all my other senses. Only a few shrubs separated us and some atavistic survival instinct took over. In one move, I rolled onto my knees, sprung up and ran up the bank and away. Vasanth, who was not expecting me to jump up from literally under his long nose, gave a startled high-pitched squeal and backed off.

The adrenaline still pumping in my body, I started taking my overdue photographs of the elephant. After a brief look at us standing on the road above him, and sniffing in our direction with his trunk, he walked off with his ears flared, shaking his head in annoyance.

We proceeded for about half an hour when we came to a *Mallotus philippensis* (Rohini) tree whose base was strewn with fresh leaves stripped neatly from the branches. I saw broken branches that were still wet, and the bark cleanly removed. Ram Sharan, Meghraj and Govind, who were watching the whole scene unfold in less than a minute, were too dumbstruck to react. The trail I had run down had actually curved towards Vasanth, a fact that I, in my excitement at getting a chance to photograph him, had not registered.

Ram Sharan told me that Vasanth was on the edge of the bank and could have grabbed me with his trunk if he had realized I was there. Slipping and falling had been a stroke of good luck.

When I reached the Gypsy, I felt my legs turn to rubber. I sat down in the back with my whole body shaking with fear. I couldn't get back on my feet for nearly half an hour. The assistants gave me water and calmed me. We abandoned tracking for the day.

For nearly a month after this incident, I could not approach an elephant group without feeling the panic rise. Whenever we got near an elephant, my hands and legs became unsteady and my body would involuntarily start shivering.

I had learnt another important lesson in elephant research. Every time I approached elephants, I should make a quick mental map of my alternative escape routes should there be an unexpected charge. Taking the time to think about this every time gave me the courage to begin approaching elephants again. Soon, I became quite adept at getting close to elephants without disturbing them.

Over the next few years, I would have unparalleled access to the lives of wild Asian elephants in Rajaji and learn much about them first hand. While I had been around elephants in Mudumalai, much of my knowledge of their behaviour and ecology was by reading the works of other researchers. Now I was thrilled that I was able to learn first-hand and my knowledge about elephants was no longer just from books.

CHAPTER 6

The Rescue

One hot summer morning in 1998, after a quick breakfast of two chappatis, and a cup of tea, I headed out with Meherban and Govind to track Shahrukh. Govind dropped us off at one of the dry rau beds. As we got down from the gypsy, I turned to Govind and said, 'Go ahead and wait in the forest camp at Bam rau. We should be there in about three or four hours.'

Govind grinned back at us replying, 'I will catch a nap,' and set off in a hurry to catch up on his beauty sleep. We were envious.

Our usual way of tracking a radio-collared elephant was to drive to the place we had last seen it and try to pick up the signals from the collar. If not, we would then climb the nearest small hillock, watchtower or roof of a nearby forest camp for the telltale ping. Then we would head on foot into the forest towards it.

The transmitter in Shahrukh's collar was not functioning very well and we had a tough time getting the first signal. Sometimes, all we had to go by was a weak, single high-pitched beep similar to the one that we used to frequently hear when trying to tune in to a radio station. When we heard the signal, we headed into the forest towards the southern boundary of Rajaji.

Suddenly, I heard the sound of a vehicle coming down the road at great speed. Traffic in Rajaji was restricted to one or two vehicles a day using the forest road. Suspecting that it might be our vehicle, Meherban and I hurried back to the road. I thought Govind had seen a tusker or a group enroute to Bam and had come to get us. On reaching the road, we saw Govind turning the Gypsy back around facing Bam. Govind was overcome with excitement and blurted, 'A calf has fallen into the well in Bam rau and the forest guard wants you to come to help rescue it.'

We jumped into the Gypsy and raced to Bam. I knew the location from having passed the well numerous times during my work. Usually, Gujjar women would be drawing water from it, or occasionally also washing clothes. It was a very small and shallow well, perhaps 1.5 metres in diameter and depth. The sides had been cemented by the Gujjars.

Once in a while, I would see dung and tracks in the mud from elephants that came to drink at the well during the hot summer months.

We reached the forest camp, parked the Gypsy and hurried to the riverbed to take stock. There in the middle of the rau was a female elephant, down on one knee with her face stuck inside the well. Her teats were engorged with milk. From inside the well came the frightened squeals of a calf. The mother responded with deep comforting rumbles. She planted both her feet firmly and tried to pull the calf out, without success. Then she went back down on her knee. This went on for a while.

On the riverbank, meanwhile, there were about fifty Gujjar men, women and children, accompanied by barking bhutia (Tibetan mastiff) dogs, making a holy ruckus. The forest guard tried to shush the crowd, but they were in no mood to listen. They wanted to chase the mother elephant and try and pull the calf out so that the well became available for their use at the earliest.

Soon, some of the more impatient men started throwing stones at the elephant. None of the stones actually hit her, but they fell nearby. She was clearly getting more and more agitated by the minute. In a short while, it became too much for her to take. Leaving the calf, she charged towards the assembled crowd.

Just as she gathered speed, the calf let out an anguished trumpet which stopped her in her tracks. She rushed back to comfort the calf with more reassuring rumbles. Again, she tried desperately to pull the calf out. Again, she failed.

The forest guard and I managed to convince the Gujjar elders that the assembled crowd needed to stop shouting and throwing stones so we could concentrate on rescuing the calf. They agreed and managed to get everyone to quiet down. Everyone, that is, except the dogs.

As to coming up with a resolution to the predicament of the calf, however, we were at a loss. I turned to Govind and the forest guard and said, 'Wait here and keep an eye on the mother elephant while we do a quick reconnaissance to find the rest of the group.' The forest guard agreed. 'Okay,' he said. 'But come back fast. I don't know how long these people will keep calm.'

We quickly located the group. Not far from where we found them, we could clearly hear the rumbles and squeals of the mother elephant and her calf, but it seemed to have no impact on her family group.

A couple of them were busy feeding on a nearby *Mallotus* shrub while the others were resting. Six or seven among them had laid down to sleep!

Finding no sympathy there, Meherban and I returned to the well. As we spoke with the forest guard and Govind, a couple of the Gujjar elders joined us. We had not been away more than ten minutes, but it appeared that they were once again getting restless and starting to holler. The situation was slipping out of control.

We moved to the middle of the rau, away from the assembly on the rau bank, and discussed our options. One suicidal option suggested was that a couple of us provoke the mother to charge behind us to distract her while the others pulled the calf out of the well. Of course, the great sage who suggested the brilliant idea wasn't willing to volunteer to be the one who would provoke the elephant to charge after him. None of our options seemed remotely workable.

While we were in animated discussion, the patience of the people on the bank ran out. They started to throw stones at the elephant again. This time, she turned around in response to the stones clattering near her and charged towards them. Again, however, the calf let out a cry and she rushed back to comfort it. She was rumbling to the calf in what sounded like soft growls.

I gestured and shouted at the crowd to desist, but no one paid me any attention. The kids thought it was great fun and joined in the stone-throwing. I felt sorry for the mother as this was happening to her inside a National Park that was supposed to be her home and where she ought to be safe. Thrice more she charged and withdrew. On her fourth charge, she slipped on the loose boulders of the rau bed, falling and hitting her forehead with a sickening crunch.

I winced. This time when she got up, something snapped in her. She curled up her trunk and charged furiously at the crowd.

The next moment, there was a full-on stampede for the nearest dehra (cluster of huts) as the men, women and children pushed and shoved each other and ran for their lives. The nimble ones quickly climbed a ficus tree like large monkeys, while the rest stumbled and tripped over one another in the melee.

Gaining quickly on the crowd, the elephant reached within two or three strides from the very last person. With helpless dread, I knew there would be an ugly scene the next moment. Suddenly, three or four of the bhutia dogs rushed at the elephant, barking and snapping at her heels. Abruptly distracted, she stopped and turned around, then tried to hit the dogs with her trunk. The dogs were too nimble and ran circles around her barking. Already distressed by her calf trapped in the well, this last assault by the dogs proved too much for the poor elephant. She lost her nerve, gave up the chase and rushed off into the thick lantana bushes growing along the bank.

I heaved a sigh of relief that certain death had been averted. Then, finding poetic justice in the fact that the people in the crowd were made to run for their lives, the six of us in the middle of the rau saw the funny side of the chase and laughed loudly.

Barely ten seconds into the laugh, I heard the bushes to my left breaking from something heavy coming through. It was the elephant sliding down the bank and charging straight at us. The six of us ran in six different directions. This time it was the turn of the Gujjars hiding in the clump of ficus trees to laugh heartily.

I had run a short distance when I realized that she was heading straight to the opposite bank and was not behind us any more. With the mother having run out of sight, the forest guard, three Gujjar men and I rushed back to the well to see what we could do. Inside the well was a very wet, tired and scared little calf, standing on its hind legs and screaming weakly. The forest guard and I quickly grabbed one forefoot; two Gujjars grabbed the other, while the third grasped its trunk. We all heaved together, managing to haul it out of the well. It had not been as heavy as I imagined an elephant calf to be. Or maybe the adrenaline from all that chasing and being chased had turned us into temporary supermen.

The calf was very weak and lay there breathing on the ground next to the well. The crowd was reassembling, but this time I shouted with as much authority as I could muster to ask everyone to move back and wait to see if the mother came back. Meherban, who had my camera, was nowhere to be seen.

The minutes ticked by and the calf stayed still. I looked through the binoculars and saw its chest rise and fall in laboured breaths. Worried, I started wondering if we would have to take the calf into captivity to save it. Not the best of outcomes.

Meanwhile, Meherban reappeared with a toothy grin and my camera bag.

I asked, 'Where the hell did you disappear to?'

He replied, 'Sir, I ran for three or four minutes and reached the road. All the while I thought the elephant was coming behind me.'

The ten minutes or so that we waited seemed like an eternity. Several voices were emphatically telling me that the mother had abandoned the calf. Other voices offered to bring buffalo milk for it.

The mother then came through the shrubs on the opposite bank, slid down to the rau and rushed to her calf. She felt it gently with her trunk and then started to break branches from a nearby shrub to cover her calf with them. It was a hot and sunny day and maybe she was protecting the calf from the heat. Soon it was entirely covered with branches.

She stood over the calf rocking gently and occasionally running her trunk over the calf's body. After a few minutes, she started to prod the calf gently with her left forefoot. Within seconds, the calf stood up and a huge cheer went up in the audience.

Shortly, the mother, with calf in tow, walked slowly back towards the bank, climbed it and disappeared into the shrubs on the far side to reunite with their group. The forest filled with the noise of branches being broken and twigs eaten. All being well, we retreated to the road.

Having read about elephant behaviour and accounts of how they come to each other's rescue in times of trouble, I was a bit surprised by the group's reaction to the ordeal. They had seemed oddly relaxed and none had come to the aid of the mother or calf during the entire time. Evidently, I still had much to learn about elephant family life. As among humans, their reaction to crises probably ran the gamut from being overly solicitous to we-couldn't-give-two-hoots.

The forest guard was waiting with cups of tea for us when we rejoined him at the forest camp. As the rest of them chattered excitedly about the morning's incident, I reflected more quietly on it. It had only been one calf and its survival was not critical in the larger scheme of all things elephantine, but I felt an uncontrollable happiness inside me. I had a stupid, happy grin on my face for many days after and a happy story to share with my friends at the Institute.

CHAPTER 7

Spotting Spots

Every morning, before we started out from the field camp in Dholkhand, I would ask my assistants to climb onto the roof and check if any of the collared elephants were nearby.

Winter had come and gone and the mist was now replaced with harsh summer light. It was hot inside our renovated field station, a single-storey cement box that had been thoughtfully installed with a door and two windows for our occupation. There was a single room, a kitchen and no bathroom. This building, if it had been built in a major city, would have walked away with many design prizes. Our regular refrain was, '*Mausam andar kharab hai*' (The weather inside is very bad). It was usually much colder inside the room during the winters and in summers it was always hotter inside than outside. It made more sense, then, to sit out on the open verandah or sometimes sleep on the roof at night.

I was hoping that the elephants wouldn't be too hard to track that day. The summer heat used to give me terrible migraines, and the blurring edges of my senses indicated that a headache was imminent. I was relieved to hear that Mallika's signal was coming from a place known as Shikari Bada, a very nice and shady habitat dominated by tall sal trees, and within walking distance from the field station. We proceeded on foot, crossed the Dholkhand rau, homed in on the signal, and found the elephants feeding peacefully under the shade of the trees. Telling my assistants to stay back, I walked on ahead to observe what the elephants were feeding on. Having followed the Rajaji elephants for almost eighteen months by then, I had learnt that groups with calves are more cautious and prone to reacting aggressively when they either smelled or saw humans too close.

Every now and then, I would stop to crush a dry leaf and drop the fragments from my fingers to check wind direction and ensure that I was downwind from them. There was no wind at all, though, and the group seemed to be completely unaware that I was nearby.

Madhuri, named after yet another famous Indian actress—our heartthrob at the time—was the second oldest female in the group after

Mallika. I assumed she was either Mallika's sister or cousin. She was accompanied by her calf who was still able to shelter under her belly, which meant that it was less than a year old. Several times, the calf tried to suckle while Madhuri fed.

The forest was noisy with the sounds of breaking branches of *Mallotus*, leaves being ripped off and then the leafless terminal twigs chewed with wet, squishy elephant sounds.

Twice while following the elephant group, I encountered chital who gave short high-pitched alarm calls and rushed away, but it did not bother the elephants and they continued feeding. I sat on a fallen tree in complete peace and isolation and at regular intervals, like wildlife scientists are expected to, took notes of what they were eating. It was one of those idyllic scenes that did not deserve to be disturbed.

Suddenly, Mallika stopped feeding, froze and flared her ears. Then she emitted a low rumble. It must have been meaningful to elephants, because the group immediately erupted in a cacophony of trumpeting, growls and squeals, shattering the stillness of the forest. They crashed through the vegetation as they rushed towards Mallika.

My first thought was that the wind had changed direction and I had been detected. In one swift motion, I jumped and hid behind the nearest sal tree. The uproar got louder by the second, and at such close range, it was quite deafening. I peeked out from behind the tree with the intention of making a run for it before they decided to charge, and not leave it till too late like some of the situations I had landed myself in before.

Surprisingly though, I found the elephants facing the direction at a right angle to where I was. They had formed a tight phalanx. A sub-adult female rushed to help Madhuri protect her calf who was now sandwiched between her and Madhuri. Mallika's daughter Malavika and her son DivT stood close to their mother. They were trumpeting, sniffing the air with snaking trunks and throwing their trunks at something in the grass, then flaring their ears and shaking their great heads. It was extraordinary! I peered through my binoculars, but could not see the object of their attention because of the tall grass and *Colebrookia* shrubs. Then, the sub-adult female charged ahead a few metres. I saw a leopard stand up from its hiding spot and flee with its tail up in the air. It was my first leopard sighting in Rajaji.

The elephants kept up the trumpeting uproar for a minute or two and then calmed down somewhat. It took them another five minutes to stop rumbling and break their tight formation. Then they moved away and so did I.

The assistants were in animated conversation when I returned, and were surprised and relieved to see me, and that too smiling. When I hadn't surfaced immediately after the commotion, they had assumed the worst.

In keeping with the adage that once you see something, you see it everywhere, I started seeing leopards everywhere in Rajaji after this first eventful sighting.

Late one November evening in 1997, Yasin, Govind and I were returning to the field station from the Institute via Mohand. Just as we crossed Sukh rau, we saw a buffalo coming down the road. This was not unusual, sometimes buffaloes roamed around at night. But then, just beyond the buffalo, we caught sight of a pair of cat eyes gleaming in the headlights. Beyond that, there was another pair of eyes. Govind braked hard as we passed the buffalo and switched off the engine.

In the bright headlights, a big male leopard stood for a few seconds before sitting down on the grass verge of the road. The female behind him, only slightly more than half his height and bulk, continued to stand hesitatingly where we had first spotted her, her eyes shining green as she looked straight at us.

She slunk off into the forest, looking uneasy. The male was unconcerned, his eyes yellowish green with the black irises narrowed to tiny slits. His coat was in glossy condition with well-defined rosettes. We must have been watching him for about two minutes when we heard the rustling of dry leaves from the lantana bushes behind him. In a few seconds, the female gracefully walked out and rubbed her face against his with a loud purr. She seemed to be saying something because in response, he got up and reluctantly walked off into the bushes. She paused briefly, framed in our headlights, then followed him. To this day, exactly what it was she had whispered in his ears remains conjecture. Yasin said, 'Sir, they were definitely a mating pair. Maybe they were stalking the buffalo together and because of us, a Gujjar buffalo was saved today.' I wasn't so sure a leopard could take down a buffalo, but I had to agree with Yasin that a mating pair would be more than a match for a buffalo.

Maybe because of its secretive nature, shady reputation for picking village dogs and livestock, and occasionally becoming a man-eater, the leopard's slinky beauty is little appreciated. To me, the leopard is the most beautiful wild cat in the world.

In the winter of 1997, I had been tracking an elephant group we called the Kania group, after the nalla (a small valley) which they frequented. I spent several days trying to get a good look at them so I could count how many elephants this group had, how old they were and how many males and females it had. This total count eluded me. They seemed to know that we were after them and did their best to frustrate us. They would come to the edge of a clearing and then change their minds. Instead of coming through, they would skirt the clearing, hidden among the bushes. I would be waiting for hours for them to cross a road or a riverbed. Then late in the evening, half the group would cross while the rest would continue feeding leisurely, hidden in the forest. The remaining light would fade away and there I would be left holding a notebook with yet another incomplete count.

Over the days, the group slowly headed in the direction of the Mohand gate—always taking care to remain half-hidden in the bushes. I was at my wits' end. On the rare day that I thought the entire group might finally cross a rau or road in single file, along would come a slaphappy Gujjar herdsman with his buffaloes and that would be that. The elephants would trumpet in protest and retreat into cover. I finally caught a lucky break one evening near Sukh rau. After an hour watching them feed, I saw the herd approach the road near the rau and start to cross it. The whole group took more than two hours to cross the road, but I finally had my count—there were twenty-three elephants in all in the Kania group.

Among them, I saw a very tiny calf, probably born just the week before, being carefully shepherded by his mother and aunt across the road. With his big eyes, spiky hairdo, short trunk and unsteady gait, he looked exceedingly funny and cute.

I now understood why the elephants had been so cautious and reluctant to show themselves in the open. Wariness was the best approach for the group when protecting a baby so young since it could neither run fast nor far from humans or the occasional tiger.

I got into the Gypsy with the kind of elation a hunter feels when he catches his quarry after many days of stalking. As we started crossing Sukh rau on our way back to the field station, we saw three small animals bounding across the dry riverbed. Meghraj exclaimed, 'They look like small Indian Civet.' At this, Yasin interjected, 'No, they look like leopard cubs.'

I rummaged frantically for my binoculars. The three animals were still bounding across the boulder-strewn riverbed. They were indeed leopards—a mother followed by her two cubs.

They ran in the general direction of the rau-bank forest where we had seen the Kania group crossing. The mother bounded up the riverbank, closely followed by the first cub, and disappeared into the bushes.

The second cub had fallen behind and was nearing the bank when one of the Kania elephants, having caught the scent of the mother and first cub, trumpeted loudly. Close on its heels came roars and rumbles from the rest of the group. The cub, still on the riverbed, came to a stop at the noise, then jumped up on the raised roots of a tree on the side of the rau.

It was now about three feet above the ground, and had a look of consternation as it scanned the riverbank for elephants. Its own family had disappeared from view. One of the elephants suddenly gave out another shrill trumpet and the cub started. After a few seconds of silence, it jumped down from its perch, bounded across and jumped up the riverbank, disappearing into the same area where its mother and sibling had gone.

This unexpected sighting seemed like good compensation for what had been a frustrating week of tracking elephants. We resumed our way to the field camp at Dholkhand.

Unbelievably, as we approached Dholkhand, the air ahead was rent with persistent alarm calling by chital, langur and rhesus macaques. Perhaps another leopard? If our luck was really good, maybe even a tiger. We knew, however, that western Rajaji's tigers were very shy and normally impossible to sight. Most alarm calls near roads were for leopards. There was tense anticipation in the vehicle as we followed the road that descended into the Dholkhand rau. We stopped the car and scanned all around, hoping to detect a slight movement or the giveaway skin pattern.

Suddenly, Govind caught sight of a leopard on the road ahead, crawling across with its belly to the ground. It darted across the dry riverbed, then sat on a small rock and looked directly at us.

The light faded, but we could see it clearly in our headlights. I filmed it for a few seconds before it got up from the rock and crawled behind a log.

The chital had moved away, but were still calling in alarm. To our immediate right stood a sambar female, stock still, eyes on us, tail up and the picture of alertness.

Then the leopard darted out from behind the log, ran across the rau, crossed in front of the vehicle and headed straight for the sambar. It turned out that we had completely distracted both predator and prey. The sambar, looking at us, did not realize that the leopard was running towards her. The leopard, in her hurry to get away from us, did not realize it was about to walk into a sambar.

Five strides from the sambar, the leopard accidentally loosened a small stone. As it clattered softly, the nervous sambar belled. Sambar belling at close quarters is not the best thing for people with weak hearts. Apparently, other animals feel the same way, because the startled leopard leapt into the air and shot off like a rocket into the bushes on the riverbank.

What started as a frustrating week with the Kania herd of elephants ended very well, after all.

CHAPTER 8

Saving Kiruba

For four years, I lived in the best wildlife field station in the world, and life in Dholkhand was never boring. As I mentioned earlier, the weird thermodynamics of the building meant that I spent a lot of time sitting on the verandah, drinking numerous cups of tea and watching wildlife either go past or stop to drink or loll in the waterhole out front. Not a day went by without chital, barking deer, wild pig and sambar sightings. If we switched on our torch in response to alarm calls, some nights would reveal a leopard sitting inside the waterhole.

Elephants were regular visitors. Once in a while, a bull elephant illuminated by dim moonlight would pass by like a grey ghost. Often on hot summer nights, we would hear the squelch of water being sucked up a massive trunk and splashed over the body.

With that world outside, the one large room that quadrupled as our living room, bedroom, dining room and store room for equipment and fuel never felt too small.

When we ran out of money during renovations, the toilet and arrangements for running water received the short shrift. All water had to be brought in buckets from the main forest range office about a hundred metres away. We had no electricity, and the darkness was always well defined. While in residence at the field station, it felt like a palace. Most days, after a hard day's work and a bath at the main forest camp with its comparatively modern facilities, I would sit on 'my' verandah sipping hot tea and listen to BBC World Service on my little radio. As a result, I became very knowledgeable about world affairs. Years later, I would impress my wife with my detailed recollection of events such as the coconut-fuelled freedom movement of the Bougainville Republic that she thought obscure, never having heard of it during her insular life in a land-locked part of India. Of course, listening to the same news items some five times before I went to sleep helped commit it all to memory.

We had a well-established routine where every morning all of us would meet and receive the various daily tasks assigned to each team.

We set off by 5:30 a.m. after a hot cup of tea and a couple of rotis or bread. Most days, we would finish the tasks by early afternoon and come back to the field station for a quick lunch, and then head out again for an afternoon session of work.

In the summer of 1997, I received a message from Dr. Johnsingh that permissions to collar two more elephants had been granted by the Ministry of Environment and Forests. I was to start identifying groups from which we could collar adult females.

Western Rajaji consists of a long ridgeline running east to west. From the ridgeline, the hills run down steeply to the plains on the north and south sides. Several streams originate from near the ridge and run down either side. Many of them are dry except during the monsoon. These streams or raus, which turn into rivers during the floods, cut a wide swathe of the forests as they reach the plains.

The raus on the northern side usually had more water than the southern side during summers and drew more elephants during this time. It was May, and both our collared groups had crossed over a pass in the ridge to the northern area between the Motichur and Kans raus. We were in the area, radio tracking the elephants and identifying females from other family groups that we could potentially collar within the following week. The two selected females were large adults in two different groups. One was in a group of five comprising herself, another big female, a sub-adult female and two juveniles aged three to four years. She had a distinctive U-shaped cut on the top of her ear, which made her easily identifiable. We named her Topcut.

The other female was in a group of fifteen elephants, which included three other tall, adult females. But it was always this one female who would boldly and aggressively approach us whenever she got wind that we were near. We would later name her Diana. She had a male calf about three years old whom we named Dava.

Targets identified, I sent word to Dr. Johnsingh in Dehradun and began making logistical arrangements to get manpower from the Forest Department and the trusted captive elephants, Premkali and Arundhati.

I radio-tracked Aishwarya and Mallika's group with Meghraj, and put Ram Sharan and Ramesh on the job of keeping track of Topcut and Diana's groups. Each day, they would pick up their feeding signs from the night before and then follow the trail till they saw them. Premkali, our exceptionally brave elephant, arrived within a day.

Dr. Johnsingh and the collaring team of Dr. Goyal, Dr. Malik and a technician arrived bright and early at the Motichur Forest Rest House the next day. They were joined by Madhusudan, a WII alumnus, and my friend and forest officer Samir Sinha, who was the official appointed from the Forest Department to oversee the collaring. The assistants had been tracking the Topcut group. Within a few minutes, we drove over to Premkali, who was waiting to set off on this next adventure.

There, I double-checked the collars, removed magnets which then switched on the signal and put them away in my pocket, and ran through the tool checklist—the spare nuts, spanners, leather cutters and pliers, etc.

I then radioed the assistants, asking one of them to backtrack and show us the way. Dr. Malik carefully prepared the dart with 2.5 ml of M-99 and filled another syringe with the antidote. He then loaded the dart in the gun and handed it ceremoniously to Dr. Johnsingh, and then placed the antidote injection in a plastic case and handed it over to Dr. Goyal.

When Ram Sharan arrived, I handed the video camera to Madhusudan and climbed on Premkali with Dr. Johnsingh and Motilal, who carried a shotgun in case the elephants charged Premkali. We started off into the forest from the road with Ram Sharan leading the way on foot. The rest of the collaring team would give us a head start and then follow on foot.

After about 500 metres, we saw the elephants ahead feeding on *Ehretia* and *Mallotus* trees. The undergrowth was entirely lantana. Dr. Johnsingh asked Ram Sharan to hang back and instructed the mahout to get us closer to the group.

As Premkali pushed through, we came to a small clearing in the forest and saw three elephants. They were busy feeding and didn't seem to mind Premkali. The other members of the group were in the bushes beyond the clearing. The only elephant nearest to us, and clearly visible, was a sub-adult female. We didn't know it then, we would later name her Kiruba (Grace) once we got to know her and became aware of her incredible story. We needed a collar on only one of the individuals in a group, and since Kiruba was ideally positioned for darting, I asked Dr. Johnsingh to dart her before we lost the advantage. He took aim, pressed the trigger and the dart with its brightly-coloured tail fins hit her square on the left rump. Perfect! Or so I thought.

No one was prepared for what happened next. Kiruba trumpeted and ran. The rest of her family trumpeted loudly and rushed towards her, and they all disappeared into the lantana in a tight huddle. The hard lantana branches cracked as the elephants moved through the undergrowth ahead. All we could hear were their deep rumbles. It was our usual practice to wait for five minutes before following their trail, which we did. That is about the amount of time required for the M-99 sedative to take effect.

We moved ahead, following their trail easily. As Kiruba swayed, two big adult females stood on either side of her trying to keep her upright. The rest of the group was gathered around them. We clapped our hands and shouted to drive off the group, but they wouldn't budge. Dr. Johnsingh asked Motilal to fire his shotgun into the air. The sharp cracks from the shotgun succeeded in spooking the elephants enough to make them move away from Kiruba. What I saw at that moment made my heart sink. Kiruba had dropped to the ground on her chest, next to a small sturdy tree.

I jumped down from Premkali and did a quick inspection with Dr. Johnsingh. Luckily, her right rear foot, which had slid under her body, was keeping her belly off the ground. Though she was breathing normally, it was still not a good position for her to be in for long.

By then, the rest of the team had caught up.

I turned to Dr. Johnsingh and Dr. Goyal and asked them to give me five minutes to get the collar on Kiruba. Working rapidly, we fastened the collar. While the assistants tightened the nuts and secured the collar, I cut off the excess length with one of the machetes on hand. All the while, Madhusudan and Samir were filming the operation.

In her mouth, Kiruba still had the twigs she had been feeding on. I was a bit apprehensive when I saw this, but kept it to myself as no one else commented on it. The reason she still had the twigs in her mouth was due to the fact that she had been immobilized very quickly, an indication that we might have overdosed her.

With the collar on in record time, Dr. Goyal quickly injected the antidote into a vein in Kiruba's ear, then we moved back—me onto Premkali—and waited for her to revive. Generally, the antidote takes about five minutes to take effect, and the animal is on its feet within ten minutes. As expected, Kiruba began flapping her ears and waking up in about three or four minutes. Though she struggled to get on her feet, rocking sideways, she was unable to get up.

After a while, she rocked one more time and managed to pull her rear foot from underneath her body. But instead of standing, her chest sank to the ground. A couple of minutes passed before we realized that instead of trying to get up, she was just giving up.

Worried, I jumped down from Premkali and had a quick conversation on the walkie-talkie with Dr. Malik who was waiting at the road. He wasn't happy with the situation, and asked us to send someone to fetch an extra dose of the antidote. Ram Sharan immediately took off at top speed.

When I turned back to Kiruba, her breathing had become irregular. She was still awake, but extremely woozy. Requesting Dr. Goyal to monitor her breathing, I directed Ram Sharan and Meghraj to cut the tree against which she was leaning. The idea was to push her onto her side to relieve the pressure on her chest.

They managed to cut the tree down, but we failed to push her onto her side. She was pushing back.

Ram Sharan arrived within some minutes completely breathless. He had run the kilometre or so both ways. He handed over the plastic container containing the syringe with the antidote to Dr. Goyal, who immediately walked forward to inject her. As he held the syringe poised, his hands shook with anxiety. Taking the syringe from him, I plunged it into Kiruba's rump, emptying the antidote into her. Then with our hearts in our throats, we crossed our fingers and waited for what felt like hours, rather than the minutes that passed.

Shortly, she made as if to get up, but again failed to do so. Around me, there was loud talk about how she was dying and that there was now nothing we could do. There were arguments. Samir Sinha turned on Dr. Johnsingh and said 'Why did you dart such a young animal with a dart meant for a big adult elephant?'

Dr. Johnsingh pinned the responsibility on me, 'Christy was the one to point to the sub-adult. He said she would be okay to collar and so I went with his advice. He has been following the elephants here and should know a thing or two by now.'

Samir Sinha dismissed the explanation with, 'Christy is very young and inexperienced in immobilizing elephants. You shouldn't have listened to him.'

I felt sick to my stomach from the impending disaster. Although every tranquillizing operation comes with the risk of the animal's death, it was unthinkable to lose an elephant like this. Desperate, I walked to Kiruba and started slapping her on the side and shouting at her, '*Uth, saali, uth.*' Saali was the only mild Hindi cuss word I had picked up. I would seek Kiruba's forgiveness for it later. For now, I just wanted her to understand, take offence and get up to fight the arrogant man casting aspersions on her character.

I repeated it again and again as I slapped her repeatedly with the palm of my right hand. Her eyes rolled in fear and rage. I reached and grabbed the twigs in her mouth and jerked them out, then slapped her trunk and screamed some more, 'Come on, *uth saali, uth*.' Finally, she'd had enough. Outraged and indignant, she swung her trunk and body to hit me—and got to her feet with one swell move.

With the same momentum, I went flying backwards into the thorny lantana as her trunk whacked me across my shins and lifted me off the ground. I was pretty badly scratched, but relieved beyond belief! There was Kiruba, still woozy, but standing up unsteadily on her feet. A feeling of happiness rushed over me to see that we had managed to save her.

We left two assistants to watch over her while we returned to the rest house to freshen up and eat. Kiruba stood at the same spot for the next eight hours and then, finally, close to dusk, she walked away in the direction of her group. We celebrated with scotch and mutton curry.

The next morning, I left early to check on Kiruba, and the pings were clear and strong as we walked about half a kilometre into the forest. The group was feeding some distance away in lovely sal forest clear of undergrowth. We stood and watched. Without warning, Kiruba turned around and flared her ears. Then with a short, angry trumpet, came charging, intent on murdering me. This was no mock charge and we had no intention of standing our ground as we usually do with young elephants threatening a charge. We beat a hasty retreat to the road, grinning widely.

She had been badly insulted, and the proud lady that she was, did not intend to take it lying down. None of her family joined her in the chase. I have to say that this was one elephant charge I was happy to run from. It meant that after the dreadful fright she had given me the previous day, all was well.

The collaring team had a good laugh at breakfast over the charge. Almost immediately, we got word via wireless that Meghraj and a forest guard had located the Diana group.

Premkali was ready when we reached the spot with our gear. I opted to stay on the ground this time. Ram Sharan and Meghraj went ahead, followed by Premkali who carried Dr. Johnsingh,

A view of the rugged elephant habitat of Rajaji NP looking down from the hills around Dholkhand

The darting team led by AJT atop Premkali about to head off to start the collaring operations

Tipu waking up after being revived from the collaring operations
(Photo credit: AJT)

I am checking if Diana is fully sedated
(Photo credit: M.D. Madhusudan)

Finishing off the final touches while collaring Diana. Everyone is happy that it went without drama. (Photo credit: M.D. Madhusudan)

Seconds after I had escaped from being hit by him, I took this image of a startled Vasant (Chapter 5)

Normally docile Shahrukh, due to the onset of musth, aggressively turns around to face me as I come out of the field station

Gujjars using the well where the elephant rescue happened (Chapter 6). Inset – the actual well

Motilal and Madhusudan, with the rear guard brought up by the rest of us carrying the collars. Dr. Malik stayed with the vehicles and we promised to update him via the wireless radio.

We had walked about a kilometre before we found the group. I told Dr. Johnsingh that the female we were after was unmistakably the biggest one in the group. He located her and fired the dart at her rump, which hit her and bounced off her back. The female let out a shrill trumpet. The group commiserated with more trumpets and rumbles as they ran a short distance and stopped, all bunched together in the shade of sal trees. The rumbles and growls continued, probably to comfort the female and sound the alarm.

Madhusudan had filmed the whole sequence carefully over Dr. Johnsingh's shoulders. And once Premkali came back to where the rest of us were waiting, we quickly reviewed the video and saw that the dart had hit a pelvic bone and bounced out, spraying most of the M-99 drug into the air.

Dr. Johnsingh and Dr. Goyal felt that the amount injected was insufficient to immobilize her and radioed Dr. Malik for an extra dart with a charge of M-99. He insisted on giving it only if Dr. Goyal would personally come back to the road and take it from him.

His reluctance to hand it to anyone else was understandable. M-99 is a highly potent narcotic and can kill a human within minutes. Dr. Goyal and Ram Sharan left to collect the dart while the rest of us waited at a safe distance from the now quiet elephant herd.

Within ten minutes I heard a noise that sounded suspiciously like something heavy slipping to the ground. I rushed to a nearby tree stump and climbed it to see what had caused the noise. Diana lay on her side, surrounded by the other elephants.

Without wasting a second, Dr. Johnsingh, Motilal and I climbed on Premkali and we went through the routine of shouting, clapping and Motilal firing into the air with his shot gun. The group protested by trumpeting, but eventually moved away.

Diana was sleeping peacefully. I jumped down and prodded her with a stick to make sure that she was truly knocked out. By the time Dr. Goyal returned with the now unnecessary new dart, we had finished collaring Diana.

By now, the assistants knew what measurements to take while I made sure that the collar bolts were secured tightly. Dr. Goyal handed me the antidote, which I gave to Diana, and we then retreated to a safe distance. Only Dr. Johnsingh remained near to take some photos as she woke up.

She was up within minutes and coolly walked away to rejoin her herd. Truth be told, having lived through Kiruba's life and death drama the previous day, we were only too glad that this operation had gone like clockwork.

CHAPTER 9

Births and Rains

The rainy season was a time of complete transformation in Rajaji—a thousand little streams would blossom all over the place, and all the dry riverbeds would become fast-flowing torrents. Everything became green, and weeds proliferated in the undergrowth. Parthenium, a noxious invasive weed accidentally imported with wheat from the Americas, became so overgrown that in certain areas they could completely hide a sub-adult elephant. The elephants dispersed over a wide area, making tracking difficult. The signals became weak or non-existent, and there were times when we found the elephants entirely on blind faith and intuition.

The roads, which the heavy rains washed away, became canals for rain water. I often wondered if the contractors who aligned and built the roads here would not have been better employed building irrigation canals for the country. With no roads for the Gypsy, we were left to fumble our way across the landscape, and chased elephants around the Park with a Yamaha motorbike and four bicycles. There were stretches on the road that were well lubricated with slimy algae. We knew those stretches of road because usually the bike would go sliding across on algal power alone, on its side, with me underneath. I fell with tedious regularity. If I got through the season without permanent scars and bruises, I considered it a lucky season.

One time, I had just crossed a local equivalent of the water obstacle at a dirt bike rally and shifted into second gear when a tiny, five-striped palm squirrel darted across in front of my bike. I swerved right to avoid it, but the squirrel decided to turn back and cross the road again. Then undecided, it stopped in front of my bike and sat on the road to contemplate its future course of action.

I braked hard and went sliding on the road. Left behind in slow motion were the contents of the bike's side bag—the foot pump, puncture kits, rain trousers and assorted nuts and bolts. Also abandoned were the rim of the headlamp and some plastic from the dashboard. I collected large black bruises and Ram Sharan was incapacitated for a whole day.

Before this accident, I had a low opinion of the crash guard that the showroom guys had fitted free of cost around the front of the bike because it used to bruise my shin every time I started the bike. Our legs were spared damage only because of the same crash guard, and thenceforth it went up several notches in my esteem.

From my vantage point sprawled on the road, I cursed and questioned the ancestry of the squirrel in no small fashion and in fluent Hindi. In fact, I accused him of incest. I also assumed that any squirrel with such idiotic indecisiveness about where it wanted to go had to be a male. But squirrel induced injuries were nothing compared to what we had to endure in other more dangerous riverbeds. At the height of the rainy season, say July or August, a riverbed called the Beribada rau became a trap.

It so happens that somebody in the old days believed that building concrete causeways in the riverbeds would prevent the road from being washed away. Therefore, all of the boulder-filled riverbeds were layered with concrete during the dry season. Come monsoon, of course all of them were washed away, except for patches of concrete left behind to serve as monuments to the all-conquering humans.

In one such patch of remnant concrete causeway on Beribada, every rainy season seemed to revive a particularly lush layer of man-eating algae that was so green that it reflected like an emerald when exposed. This patch had to be negotiated with extreme care. If one did not fall into the algae's gaping mouth, it was only due to sheer luck, and was not, in any event, to be attributed to one's advanced riding skills.

One day, forgetting about the algal ambush ahead of me, I started to cross it at the breakneck speed of about fifteen kilometres per hour. As soon as I hit the patch, realizing my mistake too late, I should have maintained speed which, with any luck, might have enabled me to cross it. But my legs, completely ignoring my brain's startled scream to keep going, decided to brake. As in most such decisions in life, body parts that do not heed the brain end up causing disaster to the rest of the body.

The engine stopped. The wheels stopped. But the bike didn't. The bike slowly tilted and fell on to its side with me underneath. I had put my foot down to arrest proceedings, but it went out from under me, so I had no choice but to watch as everything in front of me shifted axis in slow motion. Finally, when everything in front of me had turned ninety degrees, the algae patch moved me across itself—on my shoulders, with the bike on top of me.

Ram Sharan, who preferred to walk when I crossed raus on my motorbike, came up behind me and was laughing so hard that it was difficult for me to keep on an indignant face full of injury. I ended up with a sprained shoulder, many cuts and bruises from the fall.

On the whole, however, the rainy season was a most productive period. Since my contact with the Institute reduced significantly during this season, I was under less pressure to file reports and accounts from the field. I had very little disturbance from outsiders, and Bivash Pandav, one of my best buddies from the Institute, came to visit. I was always very happy to see him because he brought along packets of instant Maggi noodles.

We generally live on rice, lentils and flour with vegetables while in the field camp, and get the occasional other item when someone goes in to town. My happiness at seeing the Maggi packets was, however, short lived. I found out that he had actually also taken tinned fruits when he went to visit another researcher in whom he had a one-sided romantic interest. The tinned fruits had not inspired any reciprocity of feelings.

When I heard 'tinned fruits', a luxury that I hadn't tasted in years, I got up and gave him a kick for treating our friendship as being worth only Maggi noodles. He laughed and said, 'Have you seen your face? Who in their right mind would waste good money buying tinned fruits for you?' (Somehow, we are still friends.) However, the elephants had plenty of good delicious food during this time of the year.

During this season, it was good to see the elephants consuming great amounts of green grass and bamboo leaves and shoots all day instead of the dead-looking brown bark and twigs, which they ate during the other two seasons.

Most of the males and one of the collared female groups moved to Ranipur in the south-eastern portion of the Park when the rains came. Here, the bamboo *Dendrocalamus strictus* and *Helicteres isora*, a favoured plant, grew in profusion. All of them gorged on bamboo shoots and leaves, their pelvic bones and sunken foreheads disappearing fast. I saw several adult males in this area, a few of them old acquaintances and several new.

Mallika and Kiruba's groups were very difficult to approach without them detecting my scent. When they did, they would remonstrate in no uncertain terms. And because I was literally on slippery ground, I decided not to take chances on the hill slopes and gave them a wide berth.

I was happy as long as I could see the adults and observe what they were eating. Since the undergrowth was very thick, I couldn't see the younger members of the group clearly. A few months later, I would find the reason for their wariness.

In the meantime, I procured fluorescent yellow rain suits for everyone at the field station, which kept the receivers dry enough to track elephants on rainy days. Tracking would have been an impossible task if not for the courage and dedication of my assistants.

Going into undergrowth or tall grass areas so thick that it can completely block out the light takes certain courage. We often came across fresh tiger pugmarks, and many times, one or the other of the assistants had to go tracking alone because we would be chasing six collared animals all over the place.

With the monsoon season nearing its end, I had to go to the Institute for a month to attend and present my findings at our annual research seminar. I returned to the Dholkhand field station in the beginning of October—straight into major equipment failure. Anything that could fail, dutifully failed. The weather computer, the data logger, the solar power system, the ignition of the Gypsy, the data loggers for temperature and humidity and my computer.

After struggling with the equipment for a full day, I gave up hope and went for a walk with Meghraj. My assistants had been tracking Kiruba and her group and they were nearby.

We found the group hidden in a small patch of vegetation in the middle of the Dholkhand rau opposite the field station. After more than an hour of waiting, a young male with short tusks came out of the bushes and went off into the rau for a drink. Another half hour later, the Kiruba group started emerging.

First, an adult female of around twenty-five years came to the edge of the patch and stood there for about fifteen minutes waiting for the others to join her. She had what appeared to be tears flowing from her eyes and stood with her trunk suspended down, showing no interest in her surroundings. I was worried that she might be sick.

Slowly, the rest of the group joined her. There were two tiny calves, one walking alongside Topcut and the other being shepherded by Kiruba. Both of them were exactly the same size and unsteady while walking and seemed like they had probably been born within hours of each other. They went to the rau to drink water and we returned to the field station along a longer detour to avoid disturbing the elephants.

Twinning is rare, but is reported for elephants in captivity. But that night, I kept thinking that something didn't quite add up. If the calves were twins, as it seemed, shouldn't they be trying to stay close to Topcut? Why was one calf next to Kiruba? I inferred that Kiruba was helping Topcut take care of her twins. I had seen many sub-adult females take over babysitting duties while the harried mothers fed. I had, in fact, read that elephant families are so close-knit that related females sometimes even allowed calves that were not their own to suckle.

The next afternoon, I set out with Ram Sharan and found the group again near the edge of a rau near our field station. The group emerged from the forest and walked to the middle of the rau. Topcut was in the lead with the two small calves tottering behind her, unsure of their feet on the big smooth boulders on the riverbed.

Kiruba, who was immediately behind, stopped to drink water from the stream. One of the calves went around to Topcut's left breast and started to suckle. The other calf tried to suckle from the right when Topcut suddenly turned around and roughly kicked the calf away from her. It screamed pitifully. I was stunned and angry at Topcut for hurting the calf.

Immediately, Kiruba trumpeted and rushed to the calf, then led it some distance away. She then extended her front right foot, and the little calf started suckling from her! We then heard deep rumbling going on between Kiruba and Topcut. I wondered what was being said! Probably some choice elephant expletives.

The realization dawned on me then that this was Kiruba's calf. From her size, I had assumed her to be a sub-adult, about fifteen years old. Having seen no overt signs of pregnancy, nor having looked for any, we had darted Kiruba when she was actually in an advanced state of gestation with her first calf. That single fact probably explained why she had been unable to get up during the recovery from tranquillization. From making assumptions, we had almost put two lives in danger and botched a darting operation. I resolved that in the future that I should do everything in my power to not risk the life of elephants we were darting.

There was more I would learn about elephants that season. We had been tracking nineteen identified adult females in the four collared groups. And in addition to the two newborn calves in Kiruba's group, Mallika had also given birth and there were two new additions to Aishwarya and Diana's groups. In total, we had five new births at the end of the monsoon by the month of September. Over three years, the nineteen identified females in our collared groups gave birth to thirteen calves. All calves, except one, were born at the end of September.

Counting back, and again forward from the births, interesting facts emerged. For females to give birth at the end of monsoon, after a twenty-two-month gestation, they would have mated with bulls two winters before.

The biggest males, like Tipu, came into musth in the winter (November–January). These bulls, with their proven survival skills and fitness levels, get the chance to mate with the most females. During the monsoon, females get nutritious food and put on weight and body fat. This allows them to feed their newborn calves milk rich in fat and other nutrients. Calves feeding on rich milk also have higher chances of surviving and producing offspring of their own.

Evolution was working in marvellous ways, ensuring that the best genes were passed to the next generation.

CHAPTER 10

The Bee Dance

Time flew by and I could now identify the core members of all four groups we were tracking. My notebooks filled up with accounts of their lives and their interactions with one another.

Mallika and Kiruba's families were very stable and I knew that if I saw one member, the others would not be far behind. On the other hand, Aishwarya and Diana lived in very unstable family groups, with several big adult females who would split up into and lead smaller units, but keep meeting up often.

In the months following the birth of Kiruba's calf, I used to scan the group anxiously, because her calf looked very small and she herself was a very young mother. I was not sure if the calf would survive, but my apprehensions were misplaced. The calf was growing into a playful little thing and doing very well. At six months, she was learning to feed by pulling food out of Kiruba's mouth.

Mallika also gave birth to a healthy calf in September 1997, around the same time as Kiruba and Topcut. He was growing up fast and always demanding to suckle his mother. Seeing the calves play, with their floppy trunks and wobbly legs, was one of the highlights of my day.

One would push the other from behind, then roles would be reversed. Usually, a slightly older female kept an eye on the little ones. Whenever there was a rough sparring match going on between the two older males in their group, Topcut's calf, about eighteen months old, would join in, butting one of the males from behind. It never failed to make me laugh.

Once in a while, a juvenile male would get too rough with the little calves during play and they would squeal in pain. The reaction from their mothers would be instant. They would rush at the young male and either whack him with their trunks or butt him hard and he would trumpet in fear and move away quickly. While I was suitably trained not to think of elephants as humans and attribute human reasons for the behaviours I observed, it was hard not to see the similarities. It was like human mothers or aunts putting a naughty child in its place.

We rolled out a schedule that kept us busy with little time for other things. Now and then, however, a near death experience would make us pause, and light up our lives with mirth. I shall never forget the day in April when the wild bees got Govind dancing.

The three assistants, Ramesh, Meherban and Ram Sharan, Govind the driver and I were out trying to track Mallika along the road north of the ridge running east to west. We had no luck getting a signal, so when we reached Koelpura, we stopped to use the wooden machan there for some height. The machan was built on a sal tree almost thirty-five feet above the ground and overlooked a muddy waterhole.

Ramesh and Meherban climbed up to the machan to check for radio signals while I walked to the waterhole to check for animal tracks. Govind was turning the Gypsy around, and seemed to have inadvertently exhaust-smoked a beehive on one of the trees. Bad move. Suddenly I heard a yelp of pain and looked up to see Govind swatting at a bee that had stung him. Worse move. A bee being slapped gives out scent signals that immediately bring in its brother bees in droves towards the source of the threat. Sure enough, we heard angry buzzing that got louder and louder. Ram Sharan, who was sitting in the back of the Gypsy, immediately ducked between the rear seats while I rushed back and ducked down near the rear wheel with my hands protecting the back of my neck.

The bees went for Govind's head. He tried to slap them off with violence. They, in turn, reciprocated with more violence. The more he yelped and jumped around, the more they stung him. The more they stung him, the more he hopped from one leg to another as if doing a tribal dance, and the more he howled and slapped at the bees.

I whispered loudly to him to stop waving about and to shut up and sit quiet instead of swatting at the bees. Worst move. Govind rushed around and crawled under the Gypsy, right next to me. Under there, he then proceeded to kick at the bees who were now stinging him in the legs. The angry bees then turned their attention to me. It was a pretty morbid sequence. Every time Govind kicked his leg in pain, a bee would come and sting me in redirected aggression. Each sting felt like someone was driving hot pins into my flesh. It was especially excruciating on the face.

While Govind yelped and slapped, many ideas ran through my mind. One was to rush into the muddy waterhole and temporarily drown myself.

The other was to start a fire and smoke the bees away.

I had a matchbox in one of the side pockets of my camera bag in the Gypsy. I called out to Ram Sharan to get the matchbox out and throw it to me. Miraculously, he hadn't been stung at all and had no intention of changing the status quo. In abject insubordination, he refused to do any such thing.

Underneath the Gypsy, Govind was epileptic. Around him, the bees were apoplectic. For the first time since the attack had started, I feared for our lives. There was no sign of external aid from Meherban and Ramesh either. In fact, there was no sign of them at all.

In desperation, I opened the front door of the Gypsy, grabbed my jacket and wrapped it around my face and neck. The thwarted bees swarmed on my forearms. Ram Sharan then made a sensible suggestion—that we try and drive off.

Govind latched on to the idea, and crazed by the pain he was in, he rolled out from under the Gypsy, dove in behind the steering wheel and started the Gypsy. We zoomed off.

Half a kilometre down the road, we stopped, got out and, in a frenzy, began piling green *Clerodendron* leaves in the middle of the road to build a smoky fire. I should clarify that

Clerodendron is not a prescribed species for bee smoke. It just happened to be available in plenty where we had stopped. At that moment, to me, any old green plant would have done the trick. The area around us filled with smoke and the bees dispersed in the haze.

Ramesh and Meherban strolled onto the road from the forest side, grinning widely, claiming they were coming to rescue us. Some claims are better not believed.

I stood trying to extract the white stings of the kamikaze bees from my hands and face, which were now swelling up. I looked up to see how Govind was doing and found him sprawled semi-conscious on the road. Stunned, we picked him up and put him in the Gypsy and I drove like a madman to Raiwala, the nearest town—only to find that no doctor was available at that early hour in the morning. By then, Govind had passed out.

In desperation, I called Dr. V.B. Mathur, a scientist at the Institute hoping that his wife, a doctor, could give us some emergency advice. She was not home, but Dr. Mathur told us to get to the Jolly Grant Hospital at Doiwala, half an hour away.

Once again, I raced to the hospital where they rushed Govind into emergency and administered antihistamines. After about an hour, when Govind was still unsteady but sufficiently revived, the doctors said we could take him home. As we drove back to Motichur, my right eye was swelling shut and making me see double. I kept swerving off the road like a drunk trying to avoid the ghost doubles of all the oncoming trucks and buses. I carried on to our field camp in Motichur where I crashed out on the camp cot within minutes of arriving.

On hearing of the incident, the forest range officer, Mr. Varma, brought a bottle of jungle honey, apparently the best antihistamine for bee stings. I felt better after having two spoons full and a long nap, although my face was swollen and I spoke with a lisp for a week after that.

For a long time thereafter, I always carried a matchbox in my pocket, but we never had another incident.

CHAPTER 11

Insult to Injury

I was now able to interpret some of the communication among the female elephants. If one of the elephants caught a suspicious scent, she would make a low, calm rumble to warn the others. An angry throbbing low growl would be to warn us from approaching any closer. Persistent, long rumbles that ended in a clear, deep and long grunt was to call to other members of the group not in the immediate vicinity. A short angry growl was used to put a naughty young male in the group in his place. There would have been many more calls in the infrasound spectrum that were not audible to us.

One bright moonlight winter night at the Dholkhand field station, just as we were about to go to sleep, Govind came in to say that there were elephants out front. We walked out quietly to the verandah and saw two adult females and their calves standing still. I turned on the receiver to see if it was one of our collared groups, and was surprised to catch both Mallika's and Tipu's signals. A closer look revealed that it was Madhuri leading the group.

Shortly, they started walking down the road towards the main forest camp. Mallika's signal became stronger and then she appeared walking in her usual unhurried gait with her new calf and daughter Malavika at her heel. She then stopped in front of the field station and gave a long rumble call ending with a grunt at the end. She was calling to DivT, her son who would have been six or seven years old by then and about six feet tall. There was no sign of him, nor any audible response.

She repeated the call and then moved down the road behind Madhuri and the rest of the family towards the main forest camp. Within about five minutes Tipu strode into sight, with his regal gait and white tusks gleaming in the moonlight. A few paces behind him was DivT. His tusks looked like a miniature version of Tipu's and again the thought crossed my mind that he might be Tipu's son.

Tipu came to a stop where Mallika had been standing and sniffed at the ground. DivT also stopped and waited. It was memorable sight—the tallest and oldest tusker in Rajaji standing in bright moonlight, and behind him a younger version, separated by at least four feet in height and forty years in age.

The stillness of the scene was broken by another long rumble contact call from Mallika. DivT, feeling all grown up in such imposing male company, ignored his mother's call. One more time, Mallika called. Again, DivT refused to respond. Enough was enough. Mallika, from near the main forest camp, growled angrily. The annoyed mother's you-will-come-here-right-now was unmistakable. The very next moment, DivT—all bravado gone, gave a short, frightened trumpet and scampered at full speed past Tipu to report to his mother. Tipu strolled leisurely after him.

That behaviour was typical of Mallika, a great matriarch who was gentle and yet firm and strong when the need arose. She was different from Diana, but was always there for her close-knit family. Diana was more fearless and always willing to split away with her children from her larger family. I never once saw Mallika alone with just her children for company. Though I loved all the elephants, I had a bit of a soft corner for Mallika. Most of what I learnt about elephant family life and behaviour was from her.

The year 1998 arrived without much ado. I made a brief Christmas visit home and returned to the field station where, between elephant tracking, I caught up on my reading.

One day, our camp cook Alam put out some table salt under the lone *Wrightia tomentosa* tree growing in the open space in front of the field station to attract the chital deer. Salt contains sodium, calcium, zinc, iron, and phosphorous that are key nutrients needed for bone and muscle growth of large mammals like elephants and deer. They are not able to meet their needs from just eating plants and hence the phenomenon of animals gathering at natural salt licks or human made salt licks as they crave for salt. Salt is often used to attract animals to a waterhole or hide in the wild in Asia and Africa. Soon, we had a herd of chital hanging about in our lawn eating the salt Alam put out.

One evening, as I sat drinking tea on the verandah with Yasin and Alam, a young tusker we called ChewChew because of his peculiar habit of making a screeching call when frightened, came to drink water at the waterhole. After quenching his thirst, he came over to the *Wrightia* tree and started to eat the salt, now mixed with soil, at the base of the tree. Yasin immediately said we could mark a scale to measure height on the tree, attract elephants to it with salt, and then measure their actual heights against it.

Shoulder height correlates with the age of elephants. This measurement has been determined through captive elephants of known ages, and up to thirty years of age; the correlation is reasonably accurate.

It was a sound idea, and I wasted no time in implementing it. I had noticed bags of animal salt lying around in the main forest camp, just a shout away. Animal salt looks pink or reddish in colour and has higher amounts of calcium, zinc, iron and other essential minerals. I fetched a bag from the forest guards and brought it to our field station kitchen, and intended to mark off height measurements on the tree that afternoon following which I'd spread the salt around the base. Before afternoon, however, our plans changed somewhat. Diana had been missing for a few days and we decided to find her first. Alam had been asking for leave, so I sent him home while we moved to Motichur to search for her north of the ridge.

It took us a couple of days to locate her in the northern sal forests. She, Dava and the calf were doing fine. Leaving Ram Sharan to continue tracking her for the next few days, I drove back to Dholkhand.

At Dholkhand, I was surprised to see many of the forest guards tumble out of their living quarters and line up with big smiles on their faces when they heard me driving in. I stopped to greet them and asked them why they looked so happy. Harpal, the one with the widest grin said, 'Sir, please go and see your condemned bungalow.' I asked, 'What do you mean?' to which he replied, 'I meant your field station is now a condemned bungalow.'

Still not understanding their joke, I drove on to the field station and was confronted with a scene of utter chaos. Mallika and her family were standing in the clearing in front of our field station with the contents of our kitchen sprawled all over it. The strong iron stove was now a flat sheet of metal, the buckets were broken and all the containers of food lay around empty.

A red fog came over me and I floored the accelerator sending the Gypsy hurtling at the elephants. They rushed off into the forest behind the field camp, protesting the unexpected intrusion with squeals and trumpets.

So that was why the forest staff at the camp had been so gleeful. Just a few days before, the forest staff had been complaining bitterly about their inability to grow any vegetables in the kitchen gardens behind their quarters because of 'my' elephants. Harpal had said, 'Sir, your elephants keep breaking our fences and eating every little thing that grows in our gardens. Do something about it.' I had laughed and replied, 'What else do you expect? The elephants have the right to eat anything that grows inside the Park.' Harpal retorted, 'Sir, you care more about the elephants than our safety and our needs.'

Now the tables had turned and I was the miserable victim. Not just that, I had to eat humble pie when, later that evening, we had to borrow food from the forest staff. Our rice, flour, lentils, cooking salt, sugar and vegetables had all been eaten by the elephants.

What had happened? In two years, they had never gone near our kitchen. I got down to investigate the crime scene and pieced the puzzle together. My first deduction was this—salt is not odourless. I had been gravely misinformed in Chemistry class. Having scavenged the salt we had left out at the foot of the tree, Mallika and Madhuri had smelled more in the kitchen. They bent the metal bars in the small kitchen window and, in the process, cracked the wall on either side of it during an attempted break-in through the window, in a manner totally unbecoming of such large ladies. Had they kept up with it, the window would have come off. But in the meantime, one of the younger elephants had discovered that it could walk onto our verandah without bumping its head on the roof. I suspected DivT, but had no concrete evidence.

He (or she) had climbed up and hit the door to the big room, making one of the door panels fall off. Perhaps the unappetizing smell of the stored petrol there had made it turn away towards the kitchen door, which it opened from the verandah. The entire door was smashed to smithereens. I found the bolt in the bolt hole with the lock intact, but otherwise there remained no evidence that a door had ever stood there.

First, they had pulled out the twenty-kilogram bag of animal salt and the adults had eaten their fill. Much salt from the torn bag was mixed underfoot with the soil in the lawn. The younger ones then started investigating other items in the kitchen. They found the stove, the vegetables, the food containers with the food and the buckets. They had even pulled out a roll of asbestos sheet we had bought to waterproof the roof, and torn it into several pieces.

We tried to clean up the mess as best as we could and I vowed never again to bring salt anywhere near the field station. Little did I know then that with one bag of salt mixed in the soil in front of the field station, I had already brought all the serious trouble from elephants as I possibly could.

Tired from the day and the clean-up, Govind and I settled down to sleep in our beds after dinner with only half a door between us and the jungle. I was just nodding off, when I heard soft footfalls of a heavy animal walking onto the field station clearing. I peered out of a side window and there was Mallika's group coming back to eat salt.

I had parked the Gypsy by the side of the building and was afraid that it would not withstand the attention of playful elephants. It was a cheap Japanese four-wheel drive that could be overturned by an elephant's little finger, so to speak, in a jiffy.

I crept quietly to the door and then launched myself onto the verandah with a blood-curdling yell. They fled immediately, with frightened squeals and much crashing into bushes. I wonder what story went out on the infrasound elephant wireless that night!

The exciting news of salt at the Institute research fellow's field station yard spread like wildfire all over Rajaji. We got elephant visitors every night. Some nights, we had visits by multiple groups or several bulls. If we were sleeping already, and missed the footfalls, we were not to worry at all. The sound of salted earth being noisily inhaled up long trunks would suffice to rouse us.

Initially, it was fun to watch the elephants that close. Also, it was quite easy to shoo them away if they went near the Gypsy. After ten days or so, however, it became much more difficult to get them to move off. We had to graduate from mere shouts to banging pots and pans. The elephants were losing all fear. One afternoon, the lantana bushes behind the camp crackled and snapped loudly. That noise always meant only one thing—elephant. Meherban and I stepped out to investigate. Around the side of the building came Amrit, a young bull about ten years old, who we knew was unusually aggressive. In previous encounters on forest trails, he would be all bluster and swagger, refusing to move away for mere mortals. From the verandah, we tried to shoo him. He simply flared his ears and charged at us. Meherban turned to run back inside. I grabbed his hand, pulled him back and took a few steps towards the charging bull, shouting loudly. Amrit stopped within trunk's reach of us, confused. Then squeaked a miserable protest and retreated. We had called his bluff. Meanwhile, Meherban shook in fear at the close call. I only hoped that

Amrit would remember this lesson and learn that charging humans might not always be the fun thing he obviously believed it was. If he ever learnt to crop-raid and made a habit of charging at villagers defending their crops, he would end up being shot by the irate villagers.

We could not leave the field station unattended, and the assistants refused to stay there alone, which meant that I could not easily get away for work. Tired of chasing elephants, I insisted on a daily rota. One morning around 7 a.m., we tracked Tipu near Mohand by the highway from Dehradun to Delhi, a distance of fourteen kilometres from Dholkhand field station as the crow flies. That night as I finished dinner, I saw a big elephant walk into the yard. In the light of my torch, I saw it was Tipu. He scraped some salt from the ground, then went on his way within five minutes.

The next morning, he was at Ranipur gate, thirty-odd kilometres from Dholkhand. He had been on a long trip, and taken a detour to check out the salt rumours for himself. It was uncanny how they all homed in on my camp. The nightly elephant visits went on for two months. Towards the end, they would barely react to our tired pot-banging. Reluctantly they might shuffle away, peering at us with their heads cocked sideways in typical elephant fashion. They had us all figured out—noisy, but ultimately ineffectual humans trying to come between them and their salt.

I was calling this battle lost from our perspective. For the first time, the term elephant–human conflict went from an abstract concept in reports and papers to something real.

A few years before, I had trekked many miles to a remote village in the Garo Hills in north-east India to investigate the death of a two-month-old human infant killed by an elephant. I reached the village and talked to various people via a translator, trying to piece together the incident. It transpired that a bull elephant had come into the village, which was a cluster of bamboo huts on stilts, looking for things to eat. It might have been the home-brewed rice beer that attracted the elephants. A general commotion started as the bull came into the village and one woman rushed out with her husband in sheer panic. Then, in a moment, she remembered that she had left her baby sleeping inside the house. Before they could turn back, the elephant had reached their little hut and pushed it down, crushing the little baby boy to death.

After putting off meeting the mother for as long as I could, I asked to talk to her. It broke my heart to see her tired and resigned eyes as she narrated the incident to me. Her pain was raw. At the end of the conversation, she asked me why I was there. I gave her the honest answer, that I was doing a survey of elephants and human-elephant conflict on behalf of Project Elephant, a government programme.

She told the forest guard, who was translating, to tell me that if people like me from Delhi (a common term referring to anyone not from north-east India) were so interested in conserving elephants, we might as well carry the elephants with us and tie them in our backyards. That comment stayed in my mind, but the significance of the words came home to me only after I had to personally face elephants all night outside my field station for two months.

We did not get a single night of restful sleep during that period and our nerves were completely frayed. All this when I was doing research on elephants and lived in a concrete field camp that could not be pushed down. I couldn't even begin to imagine the psychological impact of elephant raids on villagers living in fragile mud and bamboo huts.

Those fraught nights gave me a deeper understanding of what conflict really is all about. Providentially, the monsoon arrived and washed away all traces of the salt from our front yard.

To our great relief, the elephants finally stopped their nightly visits. Despite my deep feelings of empathy for the humans impacted, I know that it is the elephants who are losing the battle everywhere. Across Asia, their home, the forests are rapidly being cleared for human use. No one meets with elephants to get stakeholder opinion on what it's like to lose their homes.

We see crop-raiding as elephants with malignant intent to destroying our food. To the elephant, however, crop fields in the lands that used to be their forest homes, are just grasslands, only much better in taste from the millennia of human selection for nutrition and succulence of grasses like rice, sugarcane and wheat. When they attempt to use what are ethically still their homelands, they are met with bullets, arrows, molotov cocktails and in many cases, death due to poisoning.

My project goal was to study elephant behaviour, ranging patterns and populations and share the results so that the science may help in conservation decision-making. As elephants continue to die from conflict with humans, and entire parks disappear from the face of the earth, my goal continues to be to give a voice to the elephants and their right to live undisturbed on their ancestral lands.

CHAPTER 12

Elephant Courage

The Rajaji elephants were proving to be very good teachers. I was learning something new every day. They were not a uniform cast of grey animals. Far from it. Each elephant was an individual, with a unique personality. Some were so distinct that it was clearly apparent in their mien, which I learnt to 'read'. This reading and learning came to good use—I could make calculated guesses on when to stand my ground and when to run, down to the last second.

Some bulls were extremely confident and considered bluster beneath their dignity. When they were not feeling threatened or irritated, they would not mock charge. Tipu was a supreme example of the cool bull. Other bulls became nervous in the presence of humans and reacted unpredictably. Either they would charge or they would turn tail and run, making squeaking calls like an injured dog. The latter sounded particularly ridiculous coming from big bulls. Nervous elephants would also never stand still.

Although female elephants were very cautious on the whole and preferred to move away from humans, some, like Diana, would stand their ground even when alone.

I often found Diana with only her two offspring in tow—one a three-year-old male and the other a calf born in 1998. In the group of about fifteen animals of which Diana was clearly a member, I could never figure out who the matriarch was. If any of the females felt like breaking off from the larger group, they just moved from the area with only their immediate offspring. Diana was the prime example. On the other hand, Mallika and Topcut were clearly the matriarchs in their groups. They would initiate movement from one feeding site to another or towards the nearest waterhole. When other members of the group finished feeding, they would wait until their matriarch finished and signalled her readiness to get going.

From the Gujjars with their buffaloes, to grasscutters cutting *bhabar* grass for ropes to villagers looking for fodder and firewood, Rajaji was a park rife with human disturbance. The southern boundary of Rajaji was also relatively hilly and crisscrossed with boulder-filled raus, which were difficult for young calves to negotiate. Whenever a female from one of our collared groups had a new calf, therefore, they immediately moved to the northern side of the Park, which was secluded, had gentler terrain and plenty of water. There were, however, fewer fodder trees and shrubs for elephants. This meant that fewer Gujjars went there with their buffaloes, since they ate the same fodder plants as elephants. Moreover, there was no grasscutting on the northern side and there was little evidence of other disturbances. Thus, it was apparent that female elephants were trading food for safety when it was time for them to give birth or had newborns.

Winters were bitterly cold in Rajaji and in the late mornings, the elephants would climb the hills to catch some warm sun. Many days, we would ascend the hills in search of the elephants to find them sleeping peacefully in the sun near the ridges.

One November day, up on a ridge near Guleria sot, I found Mallika's group sleeping on their sides in the sun. (A sot is a narrow ravine or valley usually where the head of the dry riverbed, or the rau, starts.) After an hour of watching them, I felt sleepy myself and lay down on the grass within sight of the elephants, and fell asleep leaving Ram Sharan to watch them.

About an hour later Ram Sharan shook me awake saying the elephants were waking. I got up and watched in astonishment as one by one the entire group stood up as if in response to an internal alarm clock, stood still for a few seconds and then lay down to go back to sleep on their opposite sides.

That winter, we would often find Diana and her two calves in quiet places in the north. It was quite a challenge locating her as she would be miles away from other elephants.

One day, I tracked her deep into a sal forest where it was very quiet, a scene atypical of Rajaji. In most other areas I could always hear the Gujjars lopping trees, yelling to each other or herding their buffaloes.

It had taken us about four hours to find her and the only noise was from a few birds calling. Then I heard a branch breaking nearby. Ram Sharan and I slowly crept towards the sound and saw her standing in a small clearing, feeding on *Mallotus* twigs. Her calf looked fine and a few feet away Dava was feeding on another *Mallotus*.

After about ten minutes, she suddenly froze. She had detected our scent. Turning around slowly, she walked with her calf to Dava who, by now, had stopped feeding and turned around as well. She must have made some communication unknown to us, because the calf left her side and went over to stand next to Dava. She then started walking purposefully, but unhurriedly, to where we were standing.

We retreated down the path we had come, turned a corner and waited. After a minute or so, Diana floated into sight. She had not made a sound. There had been no breaking twigs or a loose stone being kicked or crunched under her great foot. Neither the calf nor Dava were with her.

She flared her ears, clearly indicating her displeasure at our presence in her area. Again, we retreated some distance and waited, and again she came. This went on for about ten minutes until we had moved almost half a kilometre from where she had left the calf with Dava.

Then, she stood watching us for some time before turning around and returning to her young ones.

In all likelihood, Dava would inherit his mother's confidence and one day grow up to be a dominant and fearless bull like Tipu.

That summer passed in a blur as we tracked elephants and battled through flooded raus in the subsequent monsoon. On a September day in

1998 as the monsoon was receding, we climbed a ridge above Malawali rau to encounter Mallika and her group gorging on grass.

With Mallika were her three offspring—DivT, growing to be a fine young tusker, carrying himself with a lot of confidence; Malavika, then about four years old, always sticking to her mother and being helpful in looking after the calf and watching over it while it slept, allowing Mallika to feed; and the youngest calf, a female, just under a year old, looking fat and healthy. As I sat watching them in the bright afternoon sun on that hillside, I felt life was perfect that day. It would be the last time I saw them alive.

Less than three weeks later, on 29 September 1998, forest staff woke me from deep sleep with a wireless message from Motichur. Elephants had been injured in a train accident and one of them had a collar. My heart sinking, we raced in less than an hour to Motichur in the Gypsy. I hoped against hope that it was a minor accident and stopped on the way to place a call to Dr. Johnsingh to report the matter. He said he would join me at the accident site.

At Motichur, Mallika, Malavika and the little calf all lay dead on the grassy slope next to the railway track. There was no sign of the other members of the group, including DivT. It was the bleakest day of my entire time in Rajaji. Their deaths just did not make sense to me. I could not believe that this beautiful family of elephants was gone.

Reining in my emotions, I spoke to the railway staff and forest guards there to understand how such an accident had happened. It appears that the previous night, the group had been feeding on the grass growing between the tracks, watered from the train toilets that open onto the tracks. When the train came thundering down, the calf became disoriented by the powerful headlight and noise and froze on the track. While the rest of the group hurriedly moved away, Malavika and Mallika rushed to the calf and tried to protect her from the oncoming train. The calf was killed instantaneously when the engine ran over her. Her guts lay spilled in between the tracks. The train had hit Malavika and Mallika with such force that they were thrown off the tracks. Malavika was fatally injured and died by the side of the tracks. Though severely injured, Mallika rushed back to the track trumpeting in fear and agony and reaching for her baby, trying to retrieve it from under the moving steel wheels of the train. The engine driver had braked, but the train had not come to a stop. It usually takes about 100–200 meters for a train travelling at a decent speeds to stop. Passengers said that she kept banging into the train until she could do no more and collapsed between the seventh and eight coaches. They had to bring a crane to lift her off the train and the tracks.

I felt tears well up and walked away down the tracks. All the wonderful encounters with Mallika and her offspring kept replaying in my mind. I recalled the moments when she would tenderly help her newborn calf climb the steep dry river banks by putting her trunk behind it and preventing it from slipping and falling. Elephant mothers are the best representation of courage. Mallika had paid the ultimate price in doing what she knew she must as a matriarch and mother—defend her family.

Trains have been a major killer of elephants in Rajaji and were the number one cause of elephant deaths in Rajaji in the 1990s. However, in recent years, work done by my friend Anil Singh with the Forest Department to educate and increase awareness among railway operators about elephants has paid dividends. He has worked with the drivers to create awareness about elephant behaviour and help them maintain speed limits within the Park. No Indian would ever want to be involved in the death of an elephant, and engine drivers are no exception to this feeling.

He got the railways to clear vegetation and flatten out places along the track so elephants could escape in the face of an oncoming train. Very few elephants have died since. However, across India elephants are regularly succumbing to train accidents. As trains become faster, more elephants will continue to die in such accidents without serious safety measures in place.

CHAPTER 13

Tipu, the Gentle Giant

As the winter of 1997 approached and Tipu started crop-raiding, I worried about his well-being. He was a fearless elephant and had never caused bodily harm to humans, but I did not expect people to reciprocate. They would have no qualms about resorting to lethal means to stop him from destroying their livelihood. We put extra effort into tracking him. I saw him quite a few times and enjoyed photographing him. He started spending a lot of time on the river islands of the Ganges, where the Motichur river, usually dry, meets the Ganges, there are three islands. For several years, there has been talk about this being an elephant corridor, but nothing had been done to improve its conservation status.

One afternoon, a group of people came to the corridor area carrying a dead body for cremation. They built a pyre with driftwood and the fire burnt for nearly three hours. We heard pings from

Tipu's collar. It meant he was nearby. We waited for him to emerge from the island opposite to us. The evening sun was shining in all its brightness, but it was not warming me at all.

Govind called my attention in a whisper. I was eating my packed lunch in the back of the Gypsy and looked up to see Tipu walking out from the dark interiors of the island into bright sunshine, about a 100 metres away. Instead of the thin, old version of him I'd seen a few months before, he looked robust and healthy. The collar, which a month ago was hanging loose, now seemed an exact fit around his neck.

He looked magnificent standing there in the golden light. I felt very proud of him, as though I was somehow the reason for him looking so good. It was very silly and unscientific to feel that, of course, but who can explain feelings? He drank water from the river. Each time he drank, he would twist his trunk then spray water with it like a small kid with a water pistol.

He then went and lay down in the water to take a bath. The ruddy Sheldrake ducks, which had moved away in alarm, slowly swam back past him. He immersed his gigantic body in the water and only the top of his head and eyes showed above the water level. He looked for all the world like he was enjoying the golden sunset and the colourful birds swimming past.

Then, he submerged completely, raised his trunk out of the water and sent a fine spray of water drifting upwards. Every half minute or so, he would spray the air again.

The funeral pyre had now burnt down to embers. The family members took some ash, immersed it in the river and then left after a few rituals. Tipu then emerged from the river, crossed it and passed within a few feet of the smoking cinders on his way to his nightly crop-raid. I took a very nice image of his silhouette against the purplish hue of the setting sun and we returned to the camp.

The next morning, just as I was getting ready to leave for work, I saw a forest guard running towards our field station. He was breathless by the time he reached the door. It took some time for him to regain his breath. He then told us that Tipu had been injured around midnight. He was now lying on the ground in one of the villages near Raiwala.

We hurried to the spot, reaching it in fifteen minutes, but there was no elephant in sight. His tracks headed into the forest. We picked up his trail and found him within 200 metres. He looked a bit slower than normal, but there were no signs of injury on his body. He seemed alright. Leaving Ram Sharan to stay on his trail, I went back to the village where the forest guards were there in force. The police had also arrived.

Tipu had been electrocuted. A barbed wire fence had been illegally connected to the overhead main electricity transmission line. The fence had been erected to protect a sugarcane field. The sugarcane looked ripe and almost ready for harvest. The fence showed no sign of damage, which meant that Tipu must have only touched it with the back of his trunk; but the massive jolt had struck him down. He had collapsed next to the fence.

Next to where he had fallen was a pile of his dung nearly four feet in height, probably evacuated at the time of impact. It was all partially digested vegetation and smelled very bad. He had lain unconscious from midnight till 5:30 a.m.

Tipu surviving that impact was a combination of luck, strength and experience. He was a large elephant and was in excellent physical condition. He had evidently had some experience with electrified fences because, instead of grabbing it as most elephants do, and dying as a result, he had tested it with the back of his trunk.

Still, it could very well have killed him. My skin broke out in goosebumps. The police got one of the villagers to bring a long stick and disconnected the hooks from the overhead line. They were angry because this rigged-up fence could just as well have killed an unsuspecting villager. The farmer who had erected this illegal fence had fled from the scene, and the police put out a notice to look out for him. It is a sad fact that many elephants die each year from illegally electrified fences across Asia.

Immediately after this significant incident, Tipu abandoned crop-raiding for that season. A few days later, he came into full musth, but he didn't seem to be his usual confident self. Where before he would only need to take two steps towards rival bulls before they fled, this time he was doing the retreating. We found him occasionally with a few female groups, but he did not stay with them the usual three to four days a musth bull stays with a female in heat. He also went out of musth within a month. In the previous two years, he would stay in musth for over two months.

Tipu was the biggest bull in Rajaji and he would come into musth with another two equally big bulls in the winter (November–January) and they would normally stay in musth for about forty-five days to slightly over two months. The next lot of slightly younger, but fully grown adult bulls would come into musth around February–March and would stay in musth for less than a month. The youngest bulls, who just reached adulthood, would come into musth in April–May, with their musth usually lasting only about ten to fifteen days. This made sense as most of the females in Rajaji seem to conceive in the winter when the biggest bulls are in musth.

In March 1999, I was courting a lively young woman, Kashmira, who would later be my wife. She was studying goral in Rajaji at the time. Taken with my stories of Tipu, she wanted to see him. After a failed attempt at Guleria rau, one afternoon we drove to Malawali rau where Tipu was feeding in the thick undergrowth on the bank. We scrambled down to the streambed, crouched down behind a log and waited.

As the shadows lengthened on the streambed, Tipu stepped out into the rau with slow, deliberate boss elephant steps fifteen metres ahead of us. That close, and from our squatting positions, he looked even bigger than he was. Even with my familiarity with him, or perhaps because of my anxiety at making an impression on the lady, via an elephant, Tipu's walk that day seemed particularly impressive. I felt no fear but

I could see Kashmira was completely awed and overwhelmed. As he walked away from us into the gathering dusk, scrunching the streambed pebbles softly under his massive feet, I turned around to her and asked, 'Will you marry me?'

In typical, illogical Kashmira fashion, she replied, 'I will marry Tipu.' I took that to be a yes.

After four years, as my field days on the elephant project came to a close, I worried about Tipu and wondered if he was coming to the end of his days. He was already over fifty years old and that electrocution incident had dealt him quite a blow. Kashmira talked about Tipu all the time and wanted to know every little thing about him. One evening, I made the mistake of mentioning to her my end-of-days-hypothesis. Upset, she turned to me with tears welling up in her eyes. 'How can you say such a thing? You are so cruel. I don't want him to die. In any case I don't think he will die soon.'

In what eventually became a pattern with most other predictions as well, she was right. Tipu stayed alive and well for another good eleven years.

Not long after, I prepared to leave for the University of Arizona to analyse my data and write my Ph.D. It was to be a collaboration between the Institute and the university, funded by the US Fish and Wildlife Service. Between preparations, I tried to spend as much of my last two months in the field with the elephants. I knew it was a time of my life that would never come back.

On one of those days, I was witness to an incident that drove home that Tipu was truly a gentleman.

It so happened that we were looking for elephants on the forest road between Mohand rau and Sukh rau. At one point, the signal was so strong, the receiver picked it up without antenna or cable. We parked the Gypsy and waited. Soon enough, Tipu emerged from the forest at the edge of the road just ahead. He then stepped up to a roadside puddle filled by a rain shower and drank from it. Thrilled at this photographic opportunity, I readied my camera and waited for him to cross the road.

The Gujjar men in Rajaji spent a great part of their time walking to tea stalls on the main road near Mohand, a small village near the Park gate. There to meet with their friends from other parts of the forest, they exchanged news and gossip awhile before walking or cycling back to their dehras. One of them was now walking towards us down the road, a good three hundred metres away, but steadfastly about to rain on my photo-op parade.

I whispered to Ram Sharan to wave an alert about Tipu. I watched Ram Sharan waving and then imitating an elephant with tusks. I have no idea what the man thought the motions indicated because instead of stopping, he broke into a run towards the Gypsy without so much as a glance around him. Obviously, there was only one thing on his mind—to save himself the trouble of walking all the way to Mohand by hitching a ride with us.

Immediately tense, I joined Ram Sharan in waving and then shouted to him to stop. But his mind was made up and there was no stopping him. Within the minute, he was in front of Tipu, still at his puddle by the side of the road. At the suicidal distance of five metres, the man finally turned to see what Ram Sharan had been vainly pointing to all the while. The look on his face was priceless.

I enjoy watching Tom and Jerry cartoons on television and always believed the screen actions of the characters jumping or running were grossly exaggerated. I now believe that these are based on real human actions exhibited in extreme circumstances, observed carefully by talented animators.

The man jumped straight into the air and did a ninety degree turn before his feet touched the ground. He dashed into the bushes faster than the sprinter Ben Johnson on steroids. We heard him scampering through the bushes and in a few seconds, he reappeared next to the Gypsy, out of breath. During the entire performance, all Tipu did was tilt his head and look up at the human's antics as he continued to drink water from the puddle. I guess if you've been around them for fifty years, you've seen it all.

The man panted to me in Hindi, 'Sir, God saved me today.'

I looked at him and marvelled at how he had even survived all these years in an elephant forest. I was also very mad at him. Walking straight into a tusker's face is clear threat behaviour. With that kind of provocation, if it had been any other tusker in Rajaji, the man would have been seriously injured that day, if not outright killed. Then without fail, it would have been the elephant that would have been blamed as a rogue.

I looked straight at him and said in the best Hindi I could muster, 'God has given you a pair each of eyes and ears. Why the hell can't you use them?' Tipu leisurely finished drinking, then sprayed himself to cool down in the hot afternoon sun and walked into the forest on the other side.

I hadn't managed to get a single photo. At the realization, I became even more mad at the man.

It was lucky for him that it was Tipu that afternoon and not any of the other temperamental bulls we knew in Rajaji. I didn't want the last memory of my golden time in Rajaji to have been that of an elephant attacking a man.

During the incident, Ram Sharan had noticed that Tipu's collar was fraying. Sure enough, after a couple of weeks, the collar fell off. The collar had helped us monitor Tipu's movements and observe him closely for exactly three and half years. It helped us to map his range and understand how big a forest area a bull like Tipu would need to survive. By collaring big adult bulls, we also came to understand how complex elephant behaviour was and that it was difficult to classify all elephants into a single grey lump.

Just like in humans, the elephants all had individual personalities. Some were shy. Some were bold. Some liked to roam over a wide area and some liked to roam in a much smaller area of forest. The ones who liked to roam are also the ones who have a higher chance of encountering human settlements encroaching into their forest home and, thus, learn to raid crops. We found that bulls who roamed less were more unlikely to have encountered permanent human settlements with tasty crop fields and were usually not involved in raiding crops.

The first week of June 1999 was my very last at the Dholkhand field station. We no longer had a collar on Tipu, but I wanted to take one last look at him before I left. Villagers in Soddinagar in Mohand who knew him told us that he had been seen that morning in the nearby forests.

We arrived there and soon heard the familiar sound of breaking branches. Tipu stood there, with his *makhna* friend. Not all Asian elephants have tusks. Only a proportion of Asian elephant males carry tusks and the tuskless males are called makhna. I had seen them together before. The makhna was as old as Tipu and each of the previous two summers, they had met up in this very forest block and hung out together for a week to ten days.

When two adult males meet even in non-confrontational situations, there are always subtle clues as to who is dominant. The sub-dominant male will move aside if the dominant male approaches. The relationship between Tipu and the makhna, however, seemed to be absolutely equal. They looked like they enjoyed each other's company. Once, I saw Tipu lying down and sleeping with the makhna standing nearby as if on guard. It was a fascinating relationship, and one I could only make conjectures about owing to the short window through which I was looking into the long lives of Rajaji's elephants.

My guess was that both Tipu and the makhna probably knew each other from the time when they were young bulls, just starting to leave their natal herds and explore the wilderness realms. They may have roamed together, as young males sometimes do, for ten to fifteen years. When they became fully grown adults, they would have split off to embark on their solitary lives. Once a year, perhaps their sojourns coincide in the Mohand area, or perhaps they 'plan' to meet. Then, like old buddies who go on a fishing trip or chill over beer, these two grand males catch up and spend a few days in comfortable companionship. Who knows, maybe they crack jokes or reminisce about their younger days and Rajaji's beauteous elephant ladies of yore! Then they probably slap each other on the back with their heavy trunks and rumble a 'So long then, until next year' and return to walking those jungles of their ancestors in solitude. I felt happy seeing Tipu and his friend one last time, but incredibly sad to leave all this behind and head into an unknown future.

CHAPTER 14

One Last Time

I returned from the United States after nearly a year and joined WWF International to lead their brand new conservation programme on Asian elephants and rhinos. Posted in Kathmandu, I was soon busy learning about Asian elephants across the continent and working for their conservation. My assistants in Rajaji continued work on the project, keeping a track of the elephants. Several new researchers had joined to study ungulates and vegetation ecology in Rajaji and news about Tipu and other elephants kept coming in now and then.

In 2001, the research project ended, and the assistants lost their jobs. Coincidentally at the same time, there was a spurt in elephant poaching for ivory in Corbett and Rajaji. To ensure that we kept track of the tuskers and the elephant population information in Rajaji–

Corbett, I started a new research programme to continue our work and re-hired the assistants.

I made time to visit Corbett and Rajaji in the summers every year to find out how the elephants were doing. During each visit, I would attempt to track Tipu, but never actually saw him. I had to be content with looking at his photographs taken by the assistants.

In January 2005, Bivash, who was now a faculty member at the Institute, took pictures of an elephant in the Chilla Range of Rajaji on the eastern side of the Ganges and emailed it to me with a note that this elephant seemed absolutely fearless. I had a look. It was unmistakably Tipu.

From then on, I started receiving regular pictures of Tipu from Bivash as well. Where he had only visited the forests on the eastern side of the river Ganges, an area known as Chilla, for three or four days during the time we tracked him between 1996 and 1999, it appeared that Tipu was now staying there for up to six months. He was in musth for most of that period and was seen in the company of females. We were learning that sometimes elephants can remain in musth, provided they had good body condition, for a long time (four months or more). The reason he must have moved to the Chilla side is because elephant groups do synchronize their oestrus cycle, a phenomenon true of humans as well where menstrual cycles of females living in a group eventually become synchronized. That would mean that most of the female elephants available for mating on the Rajaji side would have mated in the past two years, and he was now searching for and mating with oestrus females on the Chilla side.

By 1999, only Tipu and two other bulls were known to use the corridor between the western and eastern side of the Park across the Ganges. Females had stopped crossing the Ganges many years ago due to the disturbance created by the main road, human settlements and the railway track bisecting the corridor. So these few bulls were the only ones keeping the population genetically connected across the Ganges. Meanwhile, Rajaji had been undergoing rapid transformation. The Rajaji I had left had all kinds of human disturbance. Most of the Gujjars were poor and only had a few head of cattle. Most had upwards of four or five children, with no access to education or healthcare or any kind of governmental programmes to improve their lot. The poorer ones wanted to leave the forest to places that would provide their children more educational opportunities, and themselves another livelihood through agriculture. The richer Gujjars, of course, did not want to leave Rajaji. Some of them had buffaloes that were three or four times the officially allotted quota. Where else would you get absolutely free fodder, cheap labour from their poorer brethren and cities close by that were prepared to pay high prices for milk. In true capitalist fashion, the rich were getting richer and poor poorer. For over twenty years, Dr. Johnsingh had been writing, speaking and lobbying for the tribe to be resettled with a generous package of good agricultural land so that elephants and other wildlife in Rajaji would get some respite. His relentless pleas to create undisturbed habitats fell on the ears of some officials in the forest bureaucracy and soon a Gujjar resettlement programme started in earnest. So by 2010, over sixty per cent of the Park was free of Gujjar settlements.

On my yearly visits, I was amazed to see the Park bounce back in many different ways. In areas where the buffaloes had earlier grazed the grass to the ground and only weeds proliferated, there were now lush grasslands that are prime wildlife habitat. The body condition of the elephants on the whole seemed much better.

Rajaji was now becoming a wonderful place for elephants to live. However, this good news was tempered by the fact that the park had been hit by a spurt of tiger poaching. Most of the seven or eight tigers on the western side of Rajaji that were present when I was there fulltime, were poached. The parts from these tigers probably ended up with consumers in China, who mistakenly believe that tiger parts can cure ailments and give them strength. This resulted in a complete collapse of the tiger population on the western bank of the Ganges. The possibility of new tigers recolonizing from the Chilla side was remote as, unlike elephants, tigers did not use the corridor between Chilla and Rajaji across the Ganges due to human disturbance. When I lived there, there was not a riverbed on the Rajaji side without tiger pugmarks. Soon, only two female tigresses were surviving on the western side and pugmarks are rarely seen. Today the Uttarakhand government has started an ambitious tiger reintroduction programme and I very much hope that soon every nook and corner of western Rajaji is once again filled with tiger pugmarks like it used to be in my time.

Meanwhile, our work to create a database of identified tuskers in Rajaji progressed well. My team regularly monitored the elephant population, making ours one of the longest-running projects on Asian elephants in the wild.

Tipu had first been photographed in 1992 by Dr. Raghu Chundawat of the Institute. Of course, we hadn't known him as Tipu then. From that photograph, we had estimated his age to be about forty-five. Eighteen years after that photo, in June 2010, Bivash showed me some video footage of Tipu taken the previous winter by one of his researchers. Rewinding the clip to look closely, I realized that Tipu's right eye had completely clouded over. His left eye also looked like it was developing a cataract. He was going blind. Yet, there he was in the video, in full musth and standing majestically in the middle of the road. I longed to see him. It had been over ten years since I said goodbye, and I felt there was not much more time.

My premonition came true on the morning of 6 January 2011. In Delhi for work, I received a call from Ram Sharan saying that Tipu had been seriously injured in a fight with another bull in musth. Within minutes, Bivash called me with the same news. Cancelling my other engagements, I rushed to Rajaji the next morning.

In the forests above Motichur Rau, a forest team and the vet had already sedated Tipu so he could be treated for his injuries. He had been gored on the neck and on his trunk. I helped apply medicines on the wounds in his neck and around the head where I could reach with my height. Yes, he looked his age, but I didn't bet against him pulling through.

Even so, I knew that if he survived these wounds, there was always another bull waiting to take his place. This time, the end was near. I patted him on his trunk, not knowing what to say to an elephant as grand as him, a sage teacher and mentor to me. He was revived, but he could not move much. We left him resting. The Sultan's reign was finally coming to an end. I had the incredible good fortune to have known him, and I was able to say one last good bye.

I left. Ram Sharan and the forest staff kept a close eye on him. The next evening, 8 January 2011, Tipu walked off into the forest, stumbling into trees, blinded and unsure of his footing. He reached Motichur rau and climbed onto the railway bridge that crossed the dry rau bed.

A train was expected within a few minutes and Ram Sharan ran to the Motichur station to tell them that there was an elephant on the bridge. The train was stopped. As Ram Sharan came back, he watched in horror as Tipu tried to turn around on the narrow rail bridge, lost his footing and crashed head first into the Motichur rau bed.

The elephant mother trying desperately to pull her calf out of the well

Happy ending with elephant mother and her calf heading back to the forest after the rescue

Kiruba and Topcut with their calves feeding peacefully in the winter sun

Yasin and Govind (standing inside) inspecting the damage caused by Mallika and her family after they raided the field station for salt which can be seen spread all over the floor

Mallika and Malavika feeding on lush grass after the rainfall. The last time I saw them alive before they were killed in a train accident.

AJT inspecting Mallika and Malavika who died trying to protect Mallika's young calf who was run over by a train

Tipu at sunset after crossing the Ganges

A few days before I completed my field work and headed to the US, Tipu and I spent a couple of hours with each other near Mohand (Photo credit: K. Yoganand)

He called me on my phone, panic in his voice. I asked him to try and give Tipu some water. By the time Ram Sharan took him the water, Tipu breathed his last. Rajaji would never be the same without the Sultan's great footsteps treading across it. But there would be his legacy in the elephant steps that would follow, from the many calves he fathered over the decades.

CHAPTER 15

Reflections of a Life Well-lived

(A letter from Tipu)

If you are reading this, I must have departed for the happy grazing grounds in the sky. As one among a handful of fortunate wild elephants who lived to a ripe old age in Asia, I feel a compelling need to pass on the story of my life and the lessons I've learned from my long years roaming great distances among the sal forests and the once abundant green grasslands of Rajaji. Through the experience of a well-lived life in an ever-changing world, I express my fears and hopes for the future of all my brethren that live along the Himalayan foothills in India and Nepal.

Except for a few details like his birthplace and younger days which is based on conjecture, all others details of Tipu's story are factual.

Elephants, being wiser than humans, do not believe in the immortality of our souls and, therefore, have nothing materialistic to leave behind, except for a few words of wisdom in dealing with a world where great dangers from humans confront us. However, the majority of humans, being non-believers in the 'web of life', will collect my tusks, weigh and measure them and exhibit them or store them in dark and dusty rooms where they serve no useful purpose. In my grandmother's time, the porcupines would have a nice treat for a few weeks, chewing on and saying rude things about how distasteful I am. As the old saying goes among elephants, 'from dust we came and to dust we return'.

I was born on the hills overlooking the Ramganga river and I remember huddling under the warmth and reassuring rumbles of my extended family of aunts, cousins and, of course, my wise grandmother, a graceful doyenne, as most matriarchs are. We only met my father occasionally, especially when he was in musth. He was a fine bull feared by other elephants. Alas, his magnificent tusks and a fondness for killing human beings while crop-raiding soon caught the attention of a few pale-looking humans, wearing funny shorts and hard hats, who shot him after declaring him a rogue.

My grandmother often warned me that I inherited my fearlessness from him and predicted that my tusks would grace the living room of someone if I became reckless and killed humans. This was advice that I took to heart and, despite many grave provocations from humans, never did I retaliate in a fatal manner.

The elephants those days had vast tracts of forests and grasslands to roam, and roam we did with much abandon. We didn't meet many humans back then—apart from a few Gujjars during the winters and a few men in brown uniforms riding their cycles or going around in circles on the backs of my cousins somehow under their spell. These were very strange and frightened elephants. They rumbled in fear and rushed away as soon as we approached them. I didn't think much of them. Life, on the whole, was very peaceful.

As I became a teenager, I grew apart from my family. I spent much time with other elephant bulls my age and trailing older adult bulls and mimicking their behaviours. Soon, I felt bored with the tall grasslands along the Ramganga and migrated west to the lush grasslands along the mighty Ganges. Many herds would gather there every summer and I soon established a reputation for being a fearless young bull who, in musth, was willing to stand and fight older and bigger bulls against whom I had no chance of winning. I suffered a great many injuries and bruises, but never anything fatal. While establishing my domain on either side of the Ganga, I ran into more and more strangely behaving humans.

Some were dressed in orange clothes and some wore nothing but ashes from a fire. They would silently sit and stare vacantly into space for hours on end. For good or bad, they left us elephants alone and never showed fear or disrespect when in my presence. I felt a strange kinship with these humans. However, the humans riding a big steel monster belching black smoke and lumbering past twice a day near Motichur and Raiwala really frightened me at first. Then I soon realized that if I ignored the sound and stayed out of their way, they couldn't do me any harm. Little did I foresee that these smoking big steel 'harmless' monsters, called trains, would one day turn into elephant killers. Then, all of a sudden, things changed.

The Gujjars started to live year-round in the forest. This created great irritation for us elephants, especially me. I didn't like turning up at my favourite waterholes on a hot summer day only to find them muddied and dirty with about a dozen buffaloes wallowing in them. Some of my favourite browse trees were being lopped heavily, leaving very little for me.

Then, all of a sudden, people settled along the west bank of river Ganga and grew other varieties of grasses. They would start a fire whenever we went past their little huts to drink water from the river, but this was something that we didn't bother too much about. Soon, more huts came up near the ones already established. Before long, there were hundreds of settlers converting the lush grasslands into neatly ordered grass fields. They seemed to be very upset if we went into these grasslands for grazing. This resulted in great stress to the elephant families, especially ones with little calves who had to encounter endless commotion if they went anywhere near these settlements. We were becoming unwelcome in our own homes. What I did not understand is how suddenly humans assumed ownership of lands that we had occupied with hundreds of other creatures in perfect harmony.

It was around this time I discovered that the grass varieties humans spent hours cultivating were very tasty. This caused a great uproar among the various settlements and I was soon called everything from Ganesha to Shaitan (devil). I also discovered that humans are essentially a fearful species distrustful of every other living thing that doesn't look human. Despite all their false bravado when shouting, stone-throwing and bursting firecrackers, a mock charge was enough to clear the place of humans so I could continue feeding in peace. Eating crops made me fatter, fitter and I come into musth for longer periods of time. Soon, there was not a bull who could challenge me in Rajaji.

I courted many females and fathered many calves, many of whom have grown up in my image. Every summer, I met with my childhood friend, the great Makhna, and we spent many days in each other's company near Mohand on the Delhi–Dehradun highway. Life was not perfect, but it was not bad either. The trains had changed from harmless smoke belching slow coaches to superfast, thundering steel monsters.

Then, one winter day, my life literally turned topsy turvy. While coming back from raiding tasty sugarcane fields, I was confronted by a bunch of humans sitting on elephant back, carrying a gun. These elephants, instead of running away from me, were approaching me. Having had the bad fortune to encounter a blast from a gun, I kept a watchful eye on them. Soon I felt a hard prick on my backside followed by two more over the next few hours. I felt a little sleepy, but nothing that a nice shower from the nearest waterhole couldn't cure. I felt a little irritated at all this painful attention, but having given up on understanding human behaviour about thirty years ago, I decided to ignore the commotion.

The next morning while returning with a belly full of corncobs, I saw the same irritating elephants with humans approaching me. Shortly after receiving a painful prick, I felt very dizzy and soon fell down. When I woke up, I had this strange black thing around my neck.

Soon, I noticed a malnourished young man, usually in the company of another person, following me around regularly. Unlike other people in Rajaji, they never shouted at me or made an effort to chase me. Sometimes, we would watch each other for long periods of time. During this time, one of my favourite ladies, Mallika, and her two calves were run over tragically by the steel monster. I learnt from the other surviving members of the group that she and her older daughter died while trying to protect the youngest calf from the train.

The next year, I almost went to the happy grazing grounds when I was electrocuted one night touching an electric fence that had been connected directly to an overhead electric line. I fell down and was unconscious until sunrise. After these two incidents, I knew our world was being torn apart by forces that we could never understand. My age was beginning to tell and, for the first time, I had doubts about whether I would be able to negotiate this dangerous landscape.

Having spent many hours in the study of humans, whenever I came to a particular conclusion about their conduct, along came another who would do something unexpected to my great despair. Soon, I gave up predicting what they would do next and tried my best to lead a life of dignity. I never ran away from humans, or did I charge or chase them. Suddenly, things took a change for the better. The Gujjars were moving out of the park. It was a strange feeling to visit places within the Park that no longer resonated with the sounds of Gujjars and their cattle. I did not miss them and was content to once again have the waterholes to myself. The forests returned back to a state that I once knew, where lush green grass replaced the unpalatable weeds. The crop-raiding, along with this new flush of grass, made me come into musth for over five months.

While some problems have gone away, others are only increasing—the forests between Rajaji, my adult home, and Corbett, my birth home, are degrading very fast. At this rate, we are going to be separated forever. Yet, there are several reasons for our hopes to soar—the trains go a lot slower nowadays, a flyover is going to be built over the Chilla-Motichur corridor, which is going to become free of human habitation and the ammunition dump. I have a strong suspicion that humans are also responsible for Rajaji's renaissance, and this makes me hopeful that one day, our future generations will be able to live in harmony without conflict.

As for me, I know that my days are coming to an end. My bones feel weary and I no longer enjoy the long walks to eat crops. Younger bulls are challenging me every day. One of these days I will meet my end. When the time comes, I can hold my head high in the knowledge that I was a good ambassador for Asian elephants everywhere. I hope that the people's love and affection for me will stay in their hearts long after I am gone so they can continue to fight for our future. As the light grows dimmer, I leave with no regrets.

Acknowledgements

At the outset, I would like to dedicate this book to the memory of my late grandfather Henry Kanagasabapathy, who believed that I could achieve anything I set my mind to. I would also like to thank my parents who steadfastly supported my ambition to be a wildlife researcher when it did not look like a viable career.

This work would have been impossible but for the wonderful wild elephants with whom I spent the better part of four years in Rajaji. Males Tipu Sultan, Shahrukh, Amitab, Anand, Amrit, DivT and females Mallika, Diana, Kiruba, Aishwarya and their families have made me what I am today. I am eternally grateful to them for being patient with me and for allowing me a glimpse into the wonderful and intelligent lives they lead. I can think of no greater pleasure than to sit in the verandah of my field station sipping tea and watching the ghostly shapes of these gentle giants glide past on a moonlit night or hearing the frightened squeal of a little calf followed by the reassuring rumble of its mother.

This book would not have seen the light of day but for my wife Kashmira making me repeat the stories at endless dinners and bugging me to put it down on paper. She edited the first version and told me that my English was so bad that it would be the last time she would subject herself to self-inflicted torture like this. She of course wanted the story of Tipu, with whom she was really in love with, told. I wish to thank Tipu for convincing Kashmira to take the plunge with me.

I would be remiss if I didn't acknowledge Nilanga Jayasinghe and Giavanna Grein (Gia) who read an early manuscript, offered useful edits and made passionate pleas to get the story published and in doing so ensured that I would not drop the ball on seeing it to the final stages.

Dr. A.J.T. Johnsingh was everything a student could ask for in a supervisor. I thank him for giving me the independence to shape this work but at the same time not letting me lose sight of the overall goal of why we were doing this work. I thank Dr. Goyal for the endless cups of tea and hours of stimulating conversations about ideas on methods and analysis. I've never heard him say a single discouraging word to me. I am especially grateful to him for always letting me use all the latest technology gadgets, which he had at his disposal, and shaped my philosophy towards using and sharing the best available resources with others. Dr. Paul Krausman, Dr. Rawat, Ravi Chellam, B.C. Choudhury and Qamar Qureshi all played their parts in ensuring that I completed the work on elephants in Rajaji.

My field assistants Ramesh Chand, Ram Sharan Singh, Meghraj Saini, Meherban, Satish and driver Govind's contribution to this work cannot be measured in quantitative terms. Their tireless work in what were occasionally dangerous field conditions was amazing and I will forever remain grateful to them.

The work would not have happened but for the generosity and support of several forest officers like Mr. Vinod Rishi, late Mr. A.S. Negi, Mr. Sunil Kumar Dubey, Mr. Sameer Sinha, Mr. Sunil Pandey, Mr. Rajiv Barthari and other countless officers and staff of the Uttarakhand Forest Department.

I got through the 1990s because of friends like Ramesh, Areendran, Suresh and Ronald appearing (much against their wishes) in the 90s Williams comedy show. The quality of life in WII would have been poorer without them. I thank Udayan and Sen for helping me realize that I could also climb the Himalayan mountains. Life was one long 'Rangeela re' when they were around.

Many friends and their families (not forgetting Faculty wives) made my stay in Dehradun very memorable. I wish to thank Mrs. Johnsingh, Mrs. Rawat, Mrs. B.C., Shanti, Bhooma, Mrs. Satyakumar and Anu for inviting me into their homes and helping break the monotony of hostel food. Yashveer and Krishna, Karuna and Shilo also helped me during critical times by providing food and hours of laughter. Gandhi Doot awardee Diwakar made our life a lot less tedious. Charu and Appu made life a lot more fun during the evenings and for being such good friends.

I am truly honoured to have spent the six wonderful years in the Institute in the company of Yoganand and Pandav. It was a great journey and I enjoyed it all the way. Much to everyone's disbelief (including our own) all of us actually found people who wanted to marry us.

Many organizations were responsible in helping me work on elephants including my alma mater. The Wildlife Institute of India, the Ministry of Environment and Forests, Forest Department of Uttarakhand and the US Fish and Wildlife Service. I remain deeply grateful for their support.

Becoming a father was the best thing that happened to me. Momo (Mayon) and Popo (Luit), my two sons inspired me to be a better storyteller with their constant demand for bedtime stories. We would act out many of the stories with sounds and action. I wrote this story of my time with the elephants of Rajaji with them as the audience in mind and I hope people, young and old, get to enjoy this as much as I did reliving those days while writing this book.